National Gallery *of* Ireland
Gailearaí Náisiúnta *na* hÉireann

DIARY 2012

National Gallery *of* IRELAND

Jules Joseph Lefebvre *Lauretta,* 1870s–1880s

This painting is one of the many studies of female beauty for which Lefebvre was celebrated during his lifetime. The sprig of leaves that this girl holds resembles the laurel or bay tree, whose foliage has traditionally been employed in history to symbolise victory or distinction in the art of poetry. In portraiture, a laurel branch may imply that the sitter is a literary or artistic figure. Lefebvre was known for the precise draughtsmanship, clear contours and smooth surfaces of his work, all evident in this girl's face and profile, which are contrasted by the deep red background.

FRONT COVER Robert Ponsonby Staples
On the Beach, Broadstairs, Kent, **1899**

In this delightful painting, we see a familiar day at the seaside. Blustery weather has not deterred people from playing on the beach. A young girl walks her dog, clutching her straw hat with one hand to keep it in place. Nearby, young boys are building sand castles, while others brave the rolling waves. The sketchiness of Staples's technique perfectly captures the atmosphere. This painting may be the one exhibited as 'Our Holiday' in 1901.

Gill & Macmillan
Hume Avenue, Park West, Dublin 12
with associated companies throughout the world
www.gillmacmillan.ie

© The National Gallery of Ireland 2012
ISBN 9780717150274

Text researched and written by Sara Donaldson
Design by Tony Potter
Print origination by Teapot Press Ltd
Printed in PRC

This book is typeset in Dax

The paper used in this book comes from the wood pulp of managed forests. For every tree felled, at least one tree is planted, thereby renewing natural resources.

All rights reserved.
No part of this publication may be copied, reproduced or transmitted in any form or by any means, without permission of the publishers.

A CIP catalogue record for this book is available from the British Library.

5 4 3 2 1

2012

January • Eanáir
M	T	W	T	F	S	S
26	27	28	29	30	31	1
2	3	4	5	6	7	8
9	10	11	12	13	14	15
16	17	18	19	20	21	22
23	24	25	26	27	28	29
30	31	1	2	3	4	5

February • Feabhra
M	T	W	T	F	S	S
30	31	1	2	3	4	5
6	7	8	9	10	11	12
13	14	15	16	17	18	19
20	21	22	23	24	25	26
27	28	29	1	2	3	4

March • Márta
M	T	W	T	F	S	S
27	28	29	1	2	3	4
5	6	7	8	9	10	11
12	13	14	15	16	17	18
19	20	21	22	23	24	25
26	27	28	29	30	31	1

April • Aibreán
M	T	W	T	F	S	S
26	27	28	29	30	31	1
2	3	4	5	6	7	8
9	10	11	12	13	14	15
16	17	18	19	20	21	22
23	24	25	26	27	28	29
30						

May • Bealtaine
M	T	W	T	F	S	S
31	1	2	3	4	5	6
7	8	9	10	11	12	13
14	15	16	17	18	19	20
21	22	23	24	25	26	27
28	29	30	31	1	2	3

June • Meitheamh
M	T	W	T	F	S	S
28	29	30	31	1	2	3
4	5	6	7	8	9	10
11	12	13	14	15	16	17
18	19	20	21	22	23	24
25	26	27	28	29	30	1

July • Iúil
M	T	W	T	F	S	S
25	26	27	28	29	30	1
2	3	4	5	6	7	8
9	10	11	12	13	14	15
16	17	18	19	20	21	22
23	24	25	26	27	28	29
30	31	1	2	3	4	5

August • Lúnasa
M	T	W	T	F	S	S
30	31	1	2	3	4	5
6	7	8	9	10	11	12
13	14	15	16	17	18	19
20	21	22	23	24	25	26
27	28	29	30	31	1	2

September • Meán Fómhair
M	T	W	T	F	S	S
27	28	29	30	31	1	2
3	4	5	6	7	8	9
10	11	12	13	14	15	16
17	18	19	20	21	22	23
24	25	26	27	28	29	30

October • Deireadh Fómhair
M	T	W	T	F	S	S
1	2	3	4	5	6	7
8	9	10	11	12	13	14
15	16	17	18	19	20	21
22	23	24	25	26	27	28
29	30	31	1	2	3	4

November • Samhain
M	T	W	T	F	S	S
29	30	31	1	2	3	4
5	6	7	8	9	10	11
12	13	14	15	16	17	18
19	20	21	22	23	24	25
26	27	28	29	30	1	2

December • Nollaig
M	T	W	T	F	S	S
26	27	28	29	30	1	2
3	4	5	6	7	8	9
10	11	12	13	14	15	16
17	18	19	20	21	22	23
24	25	26	27	28	29	30
31	1	2	3	4	5	6

2013

January • Eanáir
M	T	W	T	F	S	S
31	1	2	3	4	5	6
7	8	9	10	11	12	13
14	15	16	17	18	19	20
21	22	23	24	25	26	27
28	29	30	31	1	2	3

February • Feabhra
M	T	W	T	F	S	S
28	29	30	31	1	2	3
4	5	6	7	8	9	10
11	12	13	14	15	16	17
18	19	20	21	22	23	24
25	26	27	28	1	2	3

March • Márta
M	T	W	T	F	S	S
25	26	27	28	1	2	3
4	5	6	7	8	9	10
11	12	13	14	15	16	17
18	19	20	21	22	23	24
25	26	27	28	29	30	31

April • Aibreán
M	T	W	T	F	S	S
1	2	3	4	5	6	7
8	9	10	11	12	13	14
15	16	17	18	19	20	21
22	23	24	25	26	27	28
29	30	1	2	3	4	5

May • Bealtaine
M	T	W	T	F	S	S
29	30	1	2	3	4	5
6	7	8	9	10	11	12
13	14	15	16	17	18	19
20	21	22	23	24	25	26
27	28	29	30	31	1	2

June • Meitheamh
M	T	W	T	F	S	S
27	28	29	30	31	1	2
3	4	5	6	7	8	9
10	11	12	13	14	15	16
17	18	19	20	21	22	23
24	25	26	27	28	29	30

July • Iúil
M	T	W	T	F	S	S
1	2	3	4	5	6	7
8	9	10	11	12	13	14
15	16	17	18	19	20	21
22	23	24	25	26	27	28
29	30	31	1	2	3	4

August • Lúnasa
M	T	W	T	F	S	S
29	30	31	1	2	3	4
5	6	7	8	9	10	11
12	13	14	15	16	17	18
19	20	21	22	23	24	25
26	27	28	29	30	31	1

September • Meán Fómhair
M	T	W	T	F	S	S
26	27	28	29	30	31	1
2	3	4	5	6	7	8
9	10	11	12	13	14	15
16	17	18	19	20	21	22
23	24	25	26	27	28	29
30	1	2	3	4	5	6

October • Deireadh Fómhair
M	T	W	T	F	S	S
30	1	2	3	4	5	6
7	8	9	10	11	12	13
14	15	16	17	18	19	20
21	22	23	24	25	26	27
28	29	30	31	1	2	3

November • Samhain
M	T	W	T	F	S	S
28	29	30	31	1	2	3
4	5	6	7	8	9	10
11	12	13	14	15	16	17
18	19	20	21	22	23	24
25	26	27	28	29	30	1

December • Nollaig
M	T	W	T	F	S	S
25	26	27	28	29	30	1
2	3	4	5	6	7	8
9	10	11	12	13	14	15
16	17	18	19	20	21	22
23	24	25	26	27	28	29
30	31	1	2	3	4	5

The 2012 National Gallery of Ireland Diary features a diverse selection of over fifty paintings, drawings and prints, recording landscapes, seascapes, portraits, still life, genre and historical subjects. It highlights works from the collection by Old Masters such as Guercino, Canaletto, Gainsborough and Reynolds, and by 19th- and 20th-century artists including Turner, Rossetti and Bonnard.

The Gallery's Irish collection, the largest in the world, is illustrated with paintings by some of the country's most talented artists: Thomas Roberts, Nathaniel Hone the Younger, Sarah Purser, Paul Henry, William Orpen, John Lavery and William Leech among them. Living Irish artists are also represented with portraits by Robert Ballagh and Mick O'Dea. In addition to featuring works that are well known to visitors to the Gallery, the Diary features several lesser-known paintings, prints, drawings and watercolours. Many of the works featured are recent acquisitions.

A great proportion of the Gallery's collection is available to view through its website. The online collection presents information on all acquisitions from the last ten years, as well as highlights from each of the schools of art, including many of the works featured in this Diary. The online collection will be augmented on a continual basis providing a truly invaluable resource.

Founded in 1854, the National Gallery of Ireland opened to the public ten years later. The historic parts of the building, the Dargan and Milltown Wings, are undergoing a major refurbishment project, which commenced in 2011. Throughout the term of the project the Gallery will remain open and visitors will continue to have access to the collection and research services. When completed, the refurbishment project will deliver a revitalised institution, which will provide a safe and secure home for the collection and a cultural facility that will enrich the lives of all who visit.

Nicolaes Maes, *Vertumnus and Pomona,* **1673**

In Ovid's Metamorphoses, Vertumnus, God of the Seasons, attempted to woo Pomona in various guises, finally appearing to her as an old woman. When this failed, he revealed himself to her in his true form – a youthful God – and Pomona was won over. Here Vertumnus appears in the guise of the aged woman, whose sombre clothes contrast with Pomona's fashionable red dress and wide-brimmed hat. Pomona was a skilled gardener, symbolised by the bountiful fruit basket in the foreground of the scene.

December · Nollaig

26 Monday · Luan
Saint Stephen's Day

27 Tuesday · Máirt

28 Wednesday · Céadaoin

29 Thursday · Déardaoin

30 Friday · Aoine

31 Saturday · Satharn
New Year's Eve

1 Sunday · Domhnach   **2012** January · Eanáir
New Year's Day

Govaert Flinck, *Bathsheba's Appeal to David,* **1651**

Bathsheba bore King David a son named Solomon. When she heard that Adonijah was to become king without David's knowledge, she approached her aged husband to remind him of a promise he had supposedly made, that Solomon would reign after his death. Bathsheba is shown here making her appeal, while Abishag the Shunammite, David's attendant in his old age, holds his crown and sceptre. The influence of Rembrandt, Flinck's teacher in Amsterdam, is not only apparent in the composition of the painting, but also the realism and depth of character in David's face.

M	T	W	T	F	S	S
26	27	28	1	2	3	4
5	6	7	8	9	10	11
12	13	14	15	16	17	18
19	20	21	22	23	24	25
26	27	28	29	30	31	1

January • Eanáir
Week 1 • Seachtain 1

2 Monday • Luan
Bank Holiday

3 Tuesday • Máirt
Bank Holiday Scotland

4 Wednesday • Céadaoin

5 Thursday • Déardaoin

6 Friday • Aoine

7 Saturday • Sathairn

8 Sunday • Domhnach

Ludolf Backhuysen I, *The Arrival of the 'Kattendijk' at Texel, 22 July 1702,* **1702**

The 'Kattendijk' was a 759-tonne ship of the Dutch East India Fleet, built at Zeeland in 1694 and identified here by the inscription on its stern. It returned to Holland from the East on 22 July 1702 with its fleet, another member of which, the 'Sion', can be seen to the left. The vessels are depicted arriving on the Marsdiep, a silt-free channel between the Dutch mainland and the island of Texel. In the right foreground a boat is crowded with passengers, and numerous other small vessels are shown under sail.

M	T	W	T	F	S	S
26	27	28	29	30	31	1
2	3	4	5	6	7	8
9	10	11	12	13	14	15
16	17	18	19	20	21	22
23	24	25	26	27	28	29
30	31	1	2	3	4	5

January · Eanáir
Week 2 · Seachtain 2

9 Monday · Luan

10 Tuesday · Máirt

11 Wednesday · Céadaoin

12 Thursday · Déardaoin

13 Friday · Aoine

14 Saturday · Satharn

15 Sunday · Domhnach

Seán O'Sullivan, *Portrait of Douglas Hyde (1860–1949), President of Ireland, Poet and Scholar,* **20th century**

Hyde was born in County Roscommon and studied theology and law at Trinity College Dublin. A scholar and avid promoter of the Irish language and Irish literature, he wrote poetry as well as plays for the Abbey Theatre and was co-founder and first president of the Gaelic League. He became Professor of Modern Irish at University College Dublin and was a senator of the Irish Free State on two occasions. Hyde was the first President of Ireland in 1938 and was popular in this post, holding office until his term expired in 1945.

M	T	W	T	F	S	S
26	27	28	29	30	31	1
2	3	4	5	6	7	8
9	10	11	12	13	14	15
16	17	18	19	20	21	22
23	24	25	26	27	28	29
30	31	1	2	3	4	5

January • Eanáir
Week 3 • Seachtain 3

16 Monday • Luan

17 Tuesday • Máirt

18 Wednesday • Céadaoin

19 Thursday • Déardaoin

20 Friday • Aoine

21 Saturday • Satharn

22 Sunday • Domhnach

Nicolas Lancret, *La Malice (Mischief),* **c.1735**

A young girl dozes while a mischievous boy, determined to disturb her, kneels to blow smoke into her face from a lighted roll of paper, his animated expression a counterpoint to her relaxed and sleepy features. In a dimly lit interior, the only bright colours are reserved for the girl's red bodice, blue apron and hair ribbon, and the flush of her cheek, which is echoed in the rose in her hair. With his usual light-hearted charm, Lancret has captured the innocence and gaiety of youth in this delightful composition.

M	T	W	T	F	S	S
26	27	28	29	30	31	1
2	3	4	5	6	7	8
9	10	11	12	13	14	15
16	17	18	19	20	21	22
23	24	25	26	27	28	29
30	31	1	2	3	4	5

January • Eanáir
Week 4 • Seachtain 4

23 Monday • Luan

24 Tuesday • Máirt

25 Wednesday • Céadaoin

26 Thursday • Déardaoin

27 Friday • Aoine

28 Saturday • Satharn

29 Sunday • Domhnach

Paul Henry, *The Potato Diggers,* **1912**

Henry's encounter in Paris with the work of the French Realist painter Millet inspired numerous canvases portraying potato diggers and turf cutters by the Belfast-born artitist Millet's influence is obvious in the woman bending down with her arm outstretched. The harshness of life for the peasant farmers of Achill was a theme that preoccupied Henry in the first few years following his arrival there. The picture is enlivened principally by the women's red, homespun flannel dresses which, according to the artist, 'after wear and weather and washing, turned to a variety of tones'.

M	T	W	T	F	S	S
26	27	28	29	30	31	1
2	3	4	5	6	7	8
9	10	11	12	13	14	15
16	17	18	19	20	21	22
23	24	25	26	27	28	29
30	31	1	2	3	4	5

January • Eanáir
Week 5 • Seachtain 5

30 Monday • Luan

31 Tuesday • Máirt

1 Wednesday • Céadaoin   February • Feabhra

2 Thursday • Déardaoin

3 Friday • Aoine

4 Saturday • Satharn

5 Sunday • Domhnach

Dante Gabriel Rossetti, *Jane Burden as Queen Guinevere,* **1858**

The Pre-Raphaelite artist Dante Gabriel Rossetti met the sensuously attractive Jane Burden in 1857. She became his muse and later his lover, despite her marriage to the designer William Morris. This beautiful drawing may be Rossetti's first portrait of Jane, made when she was eighteen, and it depicts her in the guise of Queen Guinevere. It is a preliminary study for one of a series of uncompleted frescos illustrating the legend of King Arthur, which were planned for the walls of the Oxford Union Society building.

M	T	W	T	F	S	S
26	27	28	29	30	31	1
2	3	4	5	6	7	8
9	10	11	12	13	14	15
16	17	18	19	20	21	22
23	24	25	26	27	28	29
30	31	1	2	3	4	5

February · Feabhra
Week 6 · Seachtain 6

6 Monday · Luan

7 Tuesday · Máirt

8 Wednesday · Céadaoin

9 Thursday · Déardaoin

10 Friday · Aoine

11 Saturday · Satharn

12 Sunday · Domhnach

Canaletto, *Saint Mark's Square, Venice,* **c.1756**

The Venetian painter Canaletto specialised in topographical *vedute* (views) of his native city, many of which depict St Mark's Square. This particular view centres on the Campanile and the Procuratie Nuove, with the Doge's Palace on the left. In order to achieve such a wide angle, the artist may have used a camera obscura – an optical device that projects a detailed image of its surroundings onto a screen. By the 18th century, portable versions allowed painters to replicate images with great precision and Canaletto is known to have used one on occasion.

M	T	W	T	F	S	S
30	31	1	2	3	4	5
6	7	8	9	10	11	12
13	14	15	16	17	18	19
20	21	22	23	24	25	26
27	28	29	1	2	3	4

February · Feabhra
Week 7 · Seachtain 7

13 Monday · Luan

14 Tuesday · Máirt
St Valentine's Day

15 Wednesday · Céadaoin

16 Thursday · Déardaoin

17 Friday · Aoine

18 Saturday · Sathairn

19 Sunday · Domhnach

Moyra Barry, *Self-Portrait in the Artist's Studio,* **1920**

Moyra Barry produced still-life pictures, landscapes, genre scenes and portraits, but specialised in flower painting. In this spirited self-portrait, she adopts a serene, if somewhat quizzical expression as she looks up from her palette. She sports a short hairstyle and wears a black scarf, tied in a flat bow, high on her head – a manner that was highly fashionable in 1920. Her delicate facial features are carefully recorded, while her smock, palette and the studio in the background are realised with more expressive and vigorous brushwork, which shows the influence of Impressionism.

M	T	W	T	F	S	S
30	31	1	2	3	4	5
6	7	8	9	10	11	12
13	14	15	16	17	18	19
20	21	22	23	24	25	26
27	28	29	1	2	3	4

February · Feabhra
Week 8 · Seachtain 8

20 Monday · Luan

21 Tuesday · Máirt

22 Wednesday · Céadaoin

23 Thursday · Déardaoin

24 Friday · Aoine

25 Saturday · Satharn

26 Sunday · Domhnach

George Leslie Hunter, *Still Life with Dahlias, Wine Glass and Fruit,* **c.1913**

A bunch of dahlias in a vase stands tall above a glass, plums, grapes, a Gallia melon and a piece of vibrant red fabric laid on a white tablecloth. Hunter's brushstrokes of thick oil paint perfectly capture the feathery quality of the dahlias' white petals and the texture of the melon skin. The black background contrasts with the bright hues of the various objects, in which Hunter demonstrates his taste for strong colour, a tendency which would ensure his membership of the Scottish Colourists in the 1920s.

M	T	W	T	F	S	S
30	31	1	2	3	4	5
6	7	8	9	10	11	12
13	14	15	16	17	18	19
20	21	22	23	24	25	26
27	28	29	1	2	3	4

February • Feabhra
Week 9 • Seachtain 9

27 Monday • Luan

28 Tuesday • Máirt

29 Wednesday • Céadaoin

1 Thursday • Déardaoin   March • Márta

2 Friday • Aoine

3 Saturday • Satharn

4 Sunday • Domhnach

Daniel Maclise, *The Marriage of Strongbow and Aoife,* **c.1854**

Maclise's exceptionally large painting depicts an event traditionally regarded as pivotal in Ireland's history. Dermot McMurrough, the King of Leinster, who had been expelled from his kingdom, sought military assistance from the Norman leader, Richard de Clare (known as Strongbow). He promised in return the hand in marriage of his daughter Aoife and his title after his death. Later generations saw this 12th-century union, shown here taking place on the battlefield at Waterford, as the first confirmation of Ireland's loss of sovereignty.

M	T	W	T	F	S	S
30	31	1	2	3	4	5
6	7	8	9	10	11	12
13	14	15	16	17	18	19
20	21	22	23	24	25	26
27	28	29	1	2	3	4

March • Márta
Week 10 • Seachtain 10

5 Monday • Luan

6 Tuesday • Máirt

7 Wednesday • Céadaoin

8 Thursday • Déardaoin

9 Friday • Aoine

10 Saturday • Satharn

11 Sunday • Domhnach

Willem Claesz. Heda, *A Banquet-piece,* **c.1635**

Light sparkles across every object in this banquet-piece, its contents observed with great precision and delicacy. The elegant pewter flagon, which was used for wine, is centrally placed between a 'Berkemeyer' glass and a 'façon de Venise'-flute glass. The latter is of an expensive type imported from Venice, but also copied in Holland. The other items are bread, a mustard pot and spoon, and two pewter plates: one with a joint of ham, the other with a knife protruding over the edge of the table, suggesting depth.

M	T	W	T	F	S	S
27	28	29	1	2	3	4
5	6	7	8	9	10	11
12	13	14	15	16	17	18
19	20	21	22	23	24	25
26	27	28	29	30	31	1

March • Márta
Week 11 • Seachtain 11

12 Monday • Luan

13 Tuesday • Máirt

14 Wednesday • Céadaoin

15 Thursday • Déardaoin

16 Friday • Aoine

17 Saturday • Satharn
St Patrick's Day

18 Sunday • Domhnach

Zanobi di Jacopo Machiavelli, *Virgin and Child Enthroned with Saints,* **c.1470**

To the left of the Virgin and Child are Saint Bernardino of Siena, holding a roundel with Christ's monogram encircled by golden rays, and Saint Mark holding his gospel. To the right are Saint Louis of Toulouse in bishop's attire and Saint Jerome holding his translation of the Bible. His cardinal's hat lies on the ground, which is holy; this is implied by the fact that the saints stand barefoot. The presence of Bernardino of Siena and Louis of Toulouse, both Franciscan saints, suggests that this altarpiece was painted for a Franciscan church.

M	T	W	T	F	S	S
27	28	29	1	2	3	4
5	6	7	8	9	10	11
12	13	14	15	16	17	18
19	20	21	22	23	24	25
26	27	28	29	30	31	1

March • Márta
Week 12 • Seachtain 12

19 Monday • Luan
Bank Holiday (RoI and NI)

20 Tuesday • Máirt

21 Wednesday • Céadaoin

22 Thursday • Déardaoin

23 Friday • Aoine

24 Saturday • Satharn

25 Sunday • Domhnach

Mick O'Dea, *Portrait of Brian Friel (b.1929), Playwright,* **2009**

This portrait was commissioned by the National Gallery of Ireland on the occasion of Brian Friel's eightieth birthday. Friel, author of *Dancing at Lughnasa* and *Philadelphia Here I Come!,* among other works, is presented in a contemplative pose. Over two days, Mick O'Dea made informal sketches of Friel at the Gresham Hotel in Dublin. One drawing captured him deep in thought, touching his fingertips together in front of his face. This pose struck O'Dea as so characteristic of Friel that he chose to use it for the final painting.

M	T	W	T	F	S	S
27	28	29	1	2	3	4
5	6	7	8	9	10	11
12	13	14	15	16	17	18
19	20	21	22	23	24	25
26	27	28	29	30	31	1

March • Márta
Week 13 • Seachtain 13

26 Monday • Luan

27 Tuesday • Máirt

28 Wednesday • Céadaoin

29 Thursday • Déardaoin

30 Friday • Aoine

31 Saturday • Satharn

1 Sunday • Domhnach   April • Aibreán

Dominicus van Wijnen, *The Temptation of Saint Anthony,* **1680s**

Saint Anthony withdrew to the desert to escape the temptations of the flesh, which he called his 'demons'. He lies beside a skull, books and candle, reminders of the transience of life. He recites his rosary, looking steadfastly at a crucifix while he is surrounded by figures embodying the seven deadly sins. The display of cosmic fireworks represents the fall of the damned and recalls passages in Saint Anthony's biography. Light bursts from a bubble, often a symbol of transience, though here it may represent the sphere of Heaven.

M	T	W	T	F	S	S
27	28	29	1	2	3	4
5	6	7	8	9	10	11
12	13	14	15	16	17	18
19	20	21	22	23	24	25
26	27	28	29	30	31	1

April • Aibreán
Week 14 • Seachtain 14

2 Monday • Luan

3 Tuesday • Máirt

4 Wednesday • Céadaoin

5 Thursday • Déardaoin

6 Friday • Aoine
Good Friday

7 Saturday • Satharn

8 Sunday • Domhnach
Easter Sunday

Harry Clarke, *The Wild Swans,* **1914–1915**

'The Wild Swans', from Hans Christian Andersen's *Fairy Tales* (1838), tells of a king's eleven sons and one daughter, Eliza, who were banished by their stepmother. The sons turned into swans and carried Eliza away on a net woven from willow and rushes. In this lyrical illustration, Eliza floats on the net, drawn along by the swans. An inscription on the back reads: ' "The Wild Swans"/The whole day they flew/onward through the air'. This drawing belongs to a series made by Harry Clarke for a deluxe edition of *Fairy Tales by Hans Christian Andersen* published by Harrap in 1916.

M	T	W	T	F	S	S
26	27	28	29	30	31	1
2	3	4	5	6	7	8
9	10	11	12	13	14	15
16	17	18	19	20	21	22
23	24	25	26	27	28	29
30						

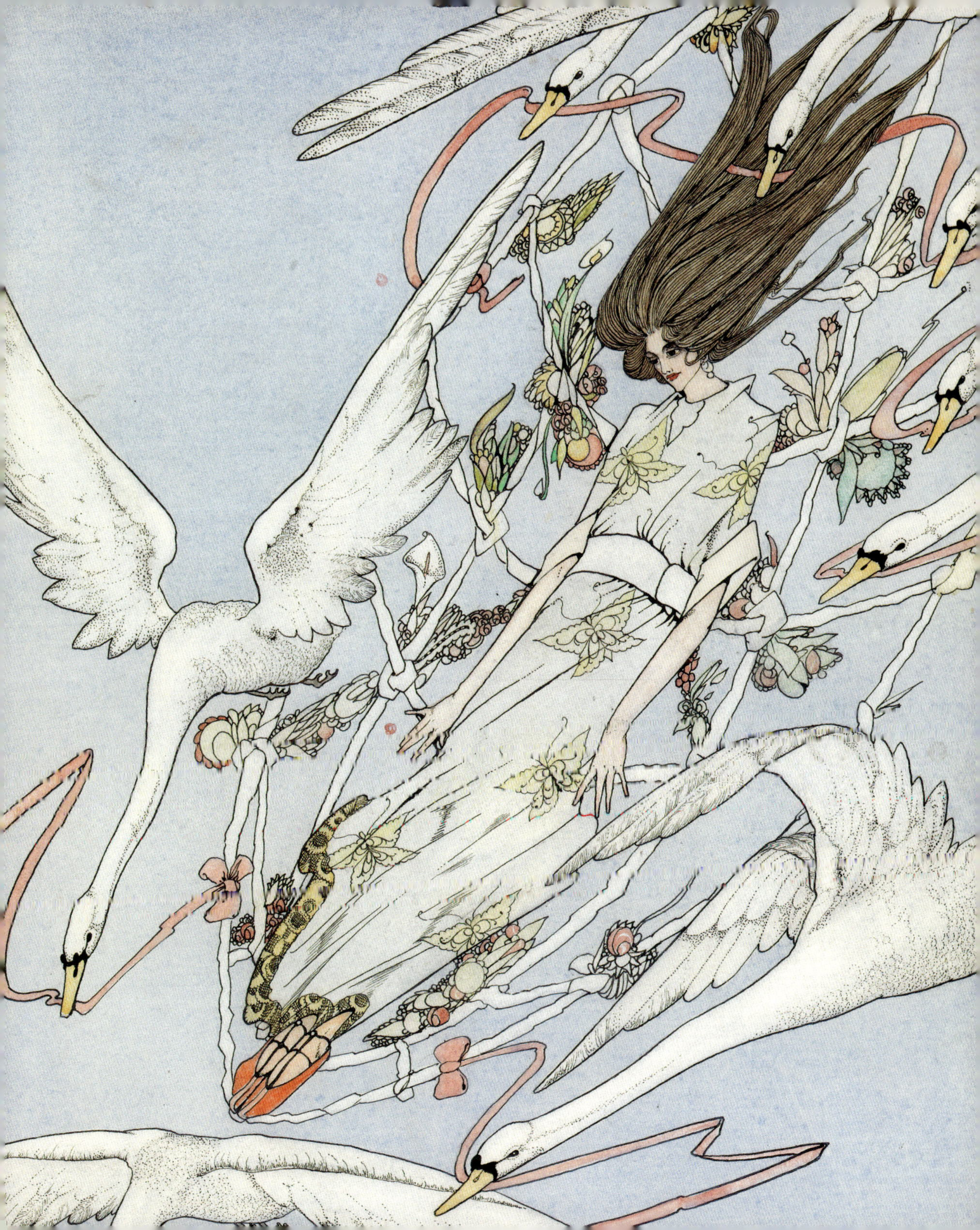

April • Aibreán
Week 15 • Seachtain 15

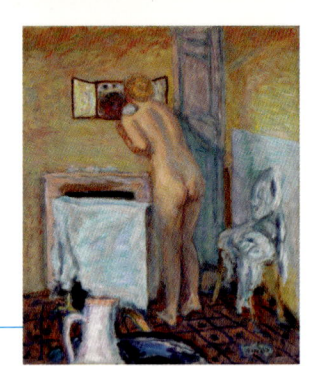

9 Monday • Luan
Easter Monday

10 Tuesday • Máirt

11 Wednesday • Céadaoin

12 Thursday • Déardaoin

13 Friday • Aoine

14 Saturday • Sathairn

15 Sunday • Domhnach

Pierre Bonnard, *Nude before a Mirror,* **1915**

The intimate subject of a nude woman at her toilette within a domestic setting was one that Bonnard explored repeatedly. While he was known to use professional models, most of his nude studies were inspired by his muse, partner and eventual wife, Marthe de Méligny. She suffered from ill heath and followed medical advice by bathing frequently, an act which Bonnard recorded in many works. In this painting the woman is captured in a private moment, looking at her face in a mirror, a reflection that is shared with the viewer.

M	T	W	T	F	S	S
26	27	28	29	30	31	1
2	3	4	5	6	7	8
9	10	11	12	13	14	15
16	17	18	19	20	21	22
23	24	25	26	27	28	29
30						

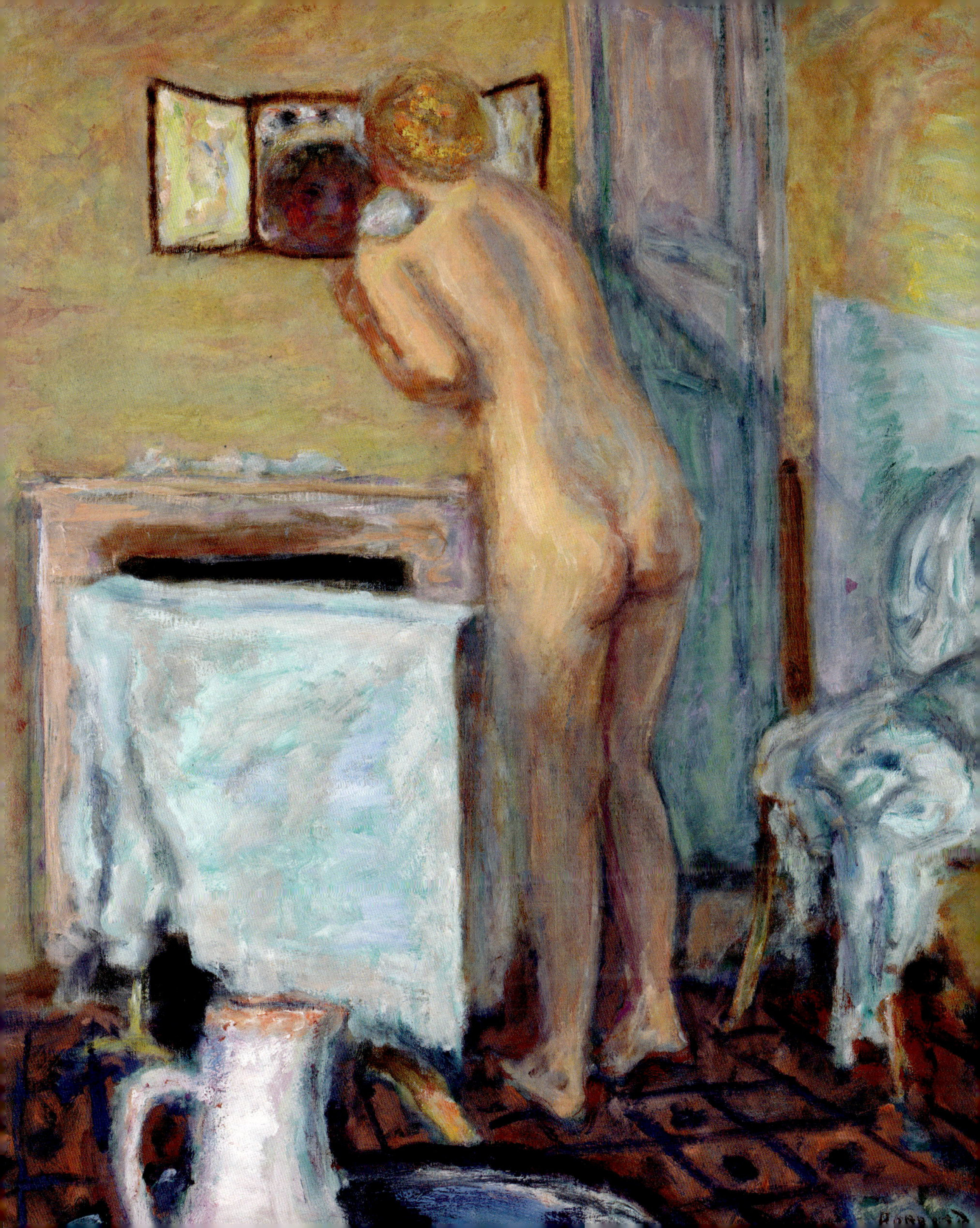

April · Aibreán
Week 16 · Seachtain 16

16 Monday · Luan

17 Tuesday · Máirt

18 Wednesday · Céadaoin

19 Thursday · Déardaoin

20 Friday · Aoine

21 Saturday · Satharn

22 Sunday · Domhnach

Nathaniel Hone the Younger, *Pastures at Malahide,* **c.1894–1896**

Under the vast expanse of a cloudy sky, cattle relax in lush grazing land in north County Dublin. Hone settled in Malahide when he returned after several years in France. In order to capture the transient effects of light, he painted rapidly, using vigorous brushstrokes and a thick application of paint, a technique that reflects his French training. He was the first Irish artist of note to train in France and this landscape is among his best-loved works.

M	T	W	T	F	S	S
26	27	28	29	30	31	1
2	3	4	5	6	7	8
9	10	11	12	13	14	15
16	17	18	19	20	21	22
23	24	25	26	27	28	29
30						

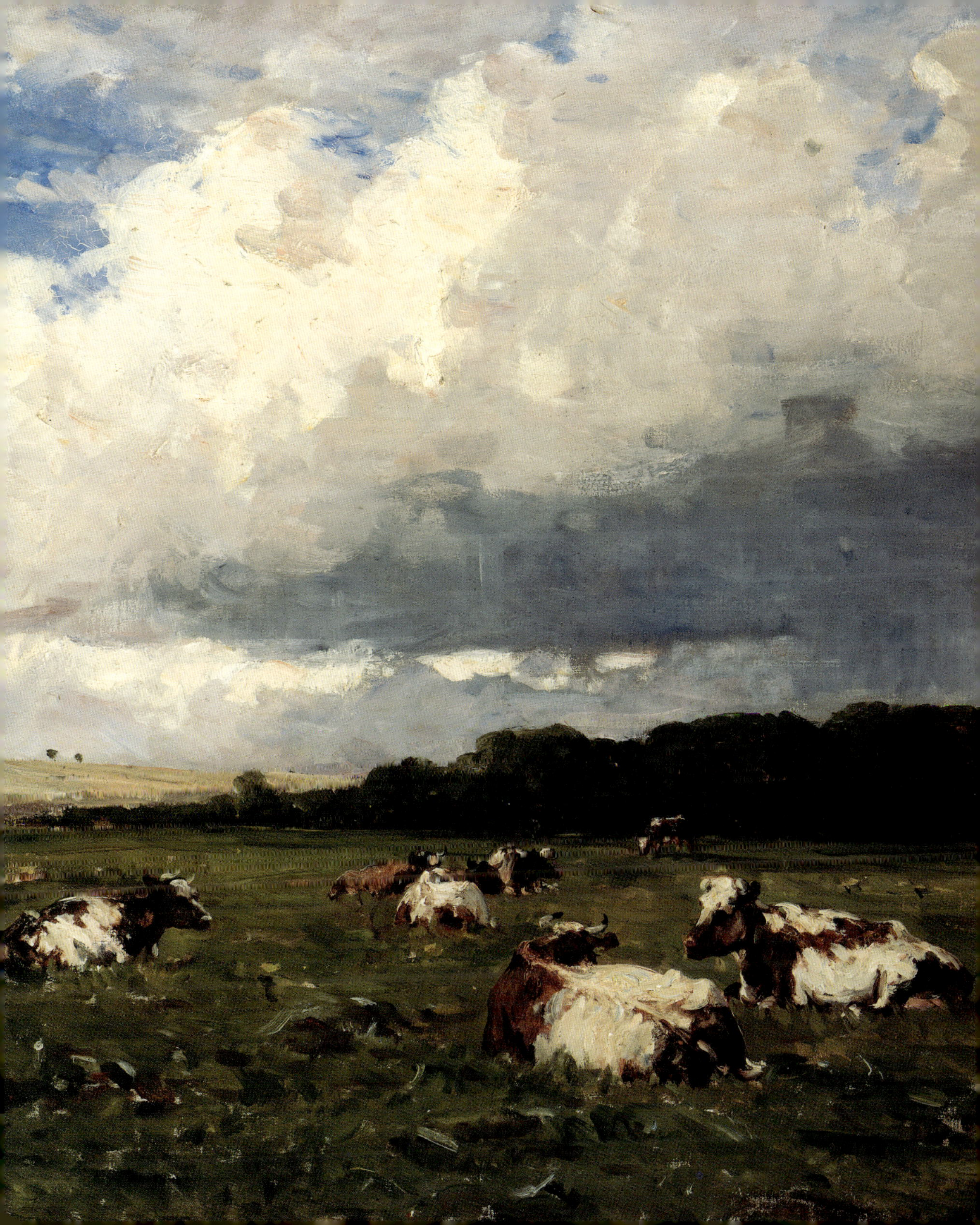

April · Aibreán
Week 17 · Seachtain 17

23 Monday · Luan

24 Tuesday · Máirt

25 Wednesday · Céadaoin

26 Thursday · Déardaoin

27 Friday · Aoine

28 Saturday · Satharn

29 Sunday · Domhnach

Studio of Peter Paul Rubens, *The Annunciation,* **1614**

As the Archangel Gabriel announces to the Virgin Mary that she will be the mother of Jesus, she turns to greet him. Her hand gesture indicates surprise, while her facial expression implies an understanding of the significance of Gabriel's message. Angels hover above in the clouds and celebrate the event by tossing flowers onto the Virgin. Along with the golden rays of light surrounding the Holy Spirit (the white dove), they add a joyous note to the painting. This work was probably painted by an assistant of Rubens under his direction.

M	T	W	T	F	S	S
26	27	28	29	30	31	1
2	3	4	5	6	7	8
9	10	11	12	13	14	15
16	17	18	19	20	21	22
23	24	25	26	27	28	29
30						

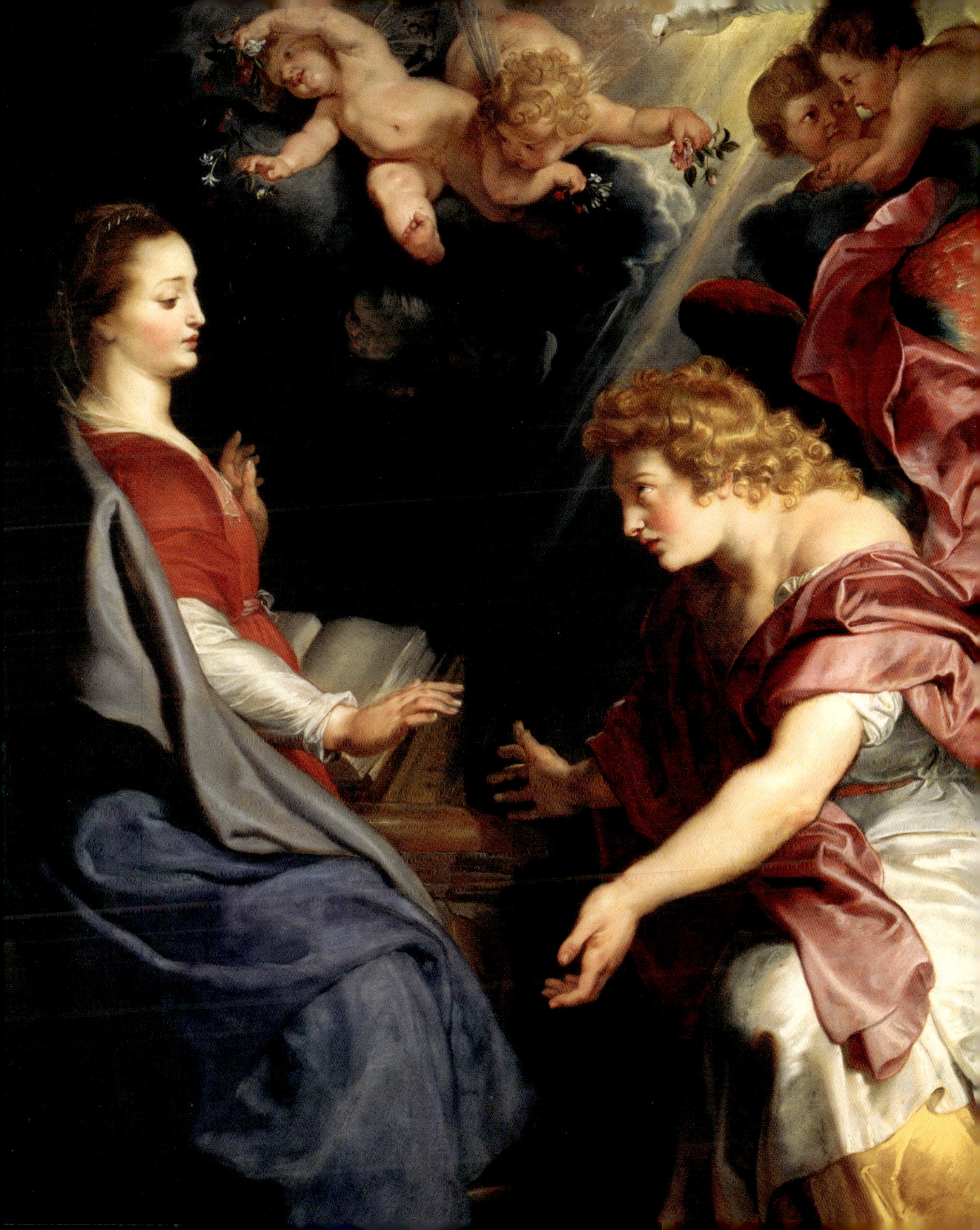

April · Aibreán
Week 18 · Seachtain 18

30 Monday · Luan

1 Tuesday · Máirt   May · Bealtaine

2 Wednesday · Céadaoin

3 Thursday · Déardaoin

4 Friday · Aoine

5 Saturday · Satharn

6 Sunday · Domhnach

François Boucher, *A Female Nude Reclining on a Chaise-Longue,* **c.1752**

Traditionally, the young girl in this provocative pose was believed to be Louise O'Murphy – a fourteen-year-old courtesan of Irish descent who became mistress to King Louis XV. The identity of the model is, however, unclear, although Louise O'Murphy is known to have modelled for Boucher, whose sensuous images of voluptuous women typify the French Rococo style of the mid-18th century. This work has a freshness that suggests it was drawn from life and is a wonderful example of Boucher's skill in depicting the female nude. Through confident strokes of chalk and graphite, he has created an image of great charm.

M	T	W	T	F	S	S
26	27	28	29	30	31	1
2	3	4	5	6	7	8
9	10	11	12	13	14	15
16	17	18	19	20	21	22
23	24	25	26	27	28	29
30						

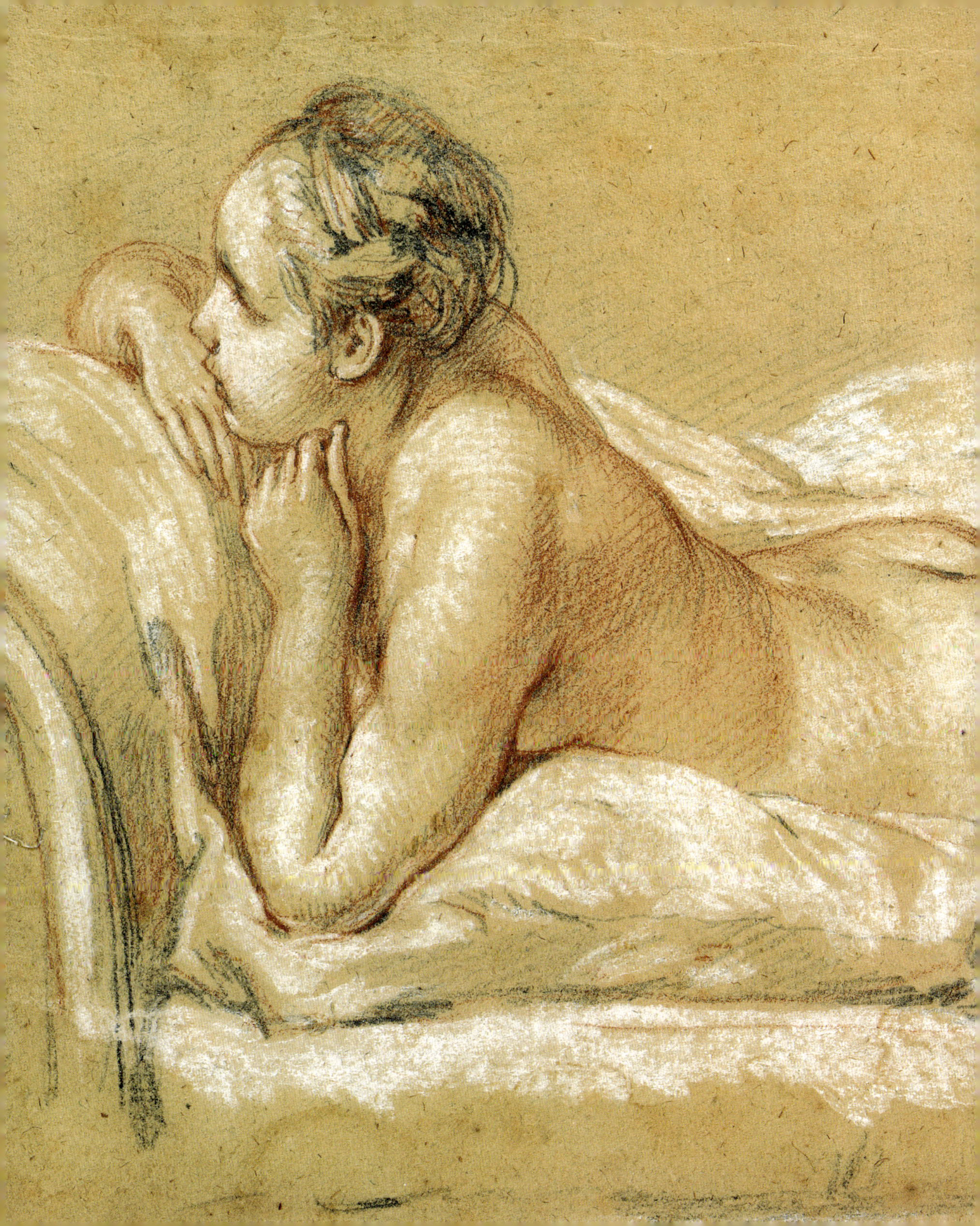

May • Bealtaine
Week 19 • Seachtain 19

7 Monday • Luan
Bank holiday (RoI and UK)

8 Tuesday • Máirt

9 Wednesday • Céadaoin

10 Thursday • Déardaoin

11 Friday • Aoine

12 Saturday • Satharn

13 Sunday • Domhnach

José Antolínez, *The Liberation of Saint Peter,* **early 1670s**

King Herod Agrippa arrested and imprisoned Saint Peter in Jerusalem for his preaching. He was bound with heavy chains and guarded by soldiers, but during the night an angel liberated him. The angel is shown waking Peter, whose chains fall from his hands. He tries to rise from his knees as he looks up at the vision with tears in his eyes. The angel's striped tunic and billowing drapery are rendered in the characteristic bright hues of Antolínez, who often combined the Venetian colouring of Titian with the swirling Baroque compositions of Rubens.

M	T	W	T	F	S	S
31	1	2	3	4	5	6
7	8	9	10	11	12	13
14	15	16	17	18	19	20
21	22	23	24	25	26	27
28	29	30	31	1	2	3

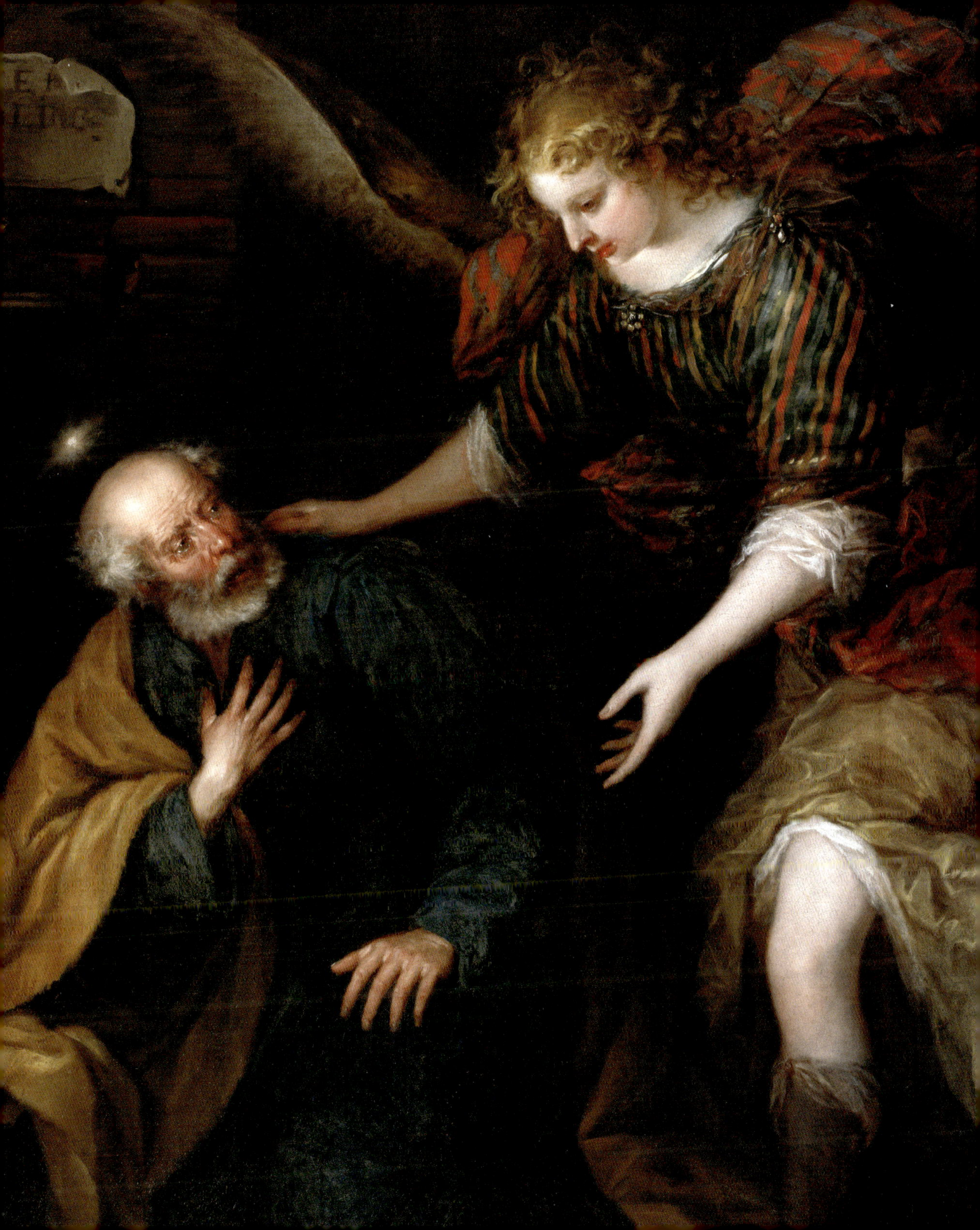

May • Bealtaine
Week 20 • Seachtain 20

14 Monday • Luan

15 Tuesday • Máirt

16 Wednesday • Céadaoin

17 Thursday • Déardaoin

18 Friday • Aoine

19 Saturday • Satharn

20 Sunday • Domhnach

Matthew James Lawless, *An Angling Party,* **c.1860**

In the centre of this group, a fashionably dressed young lady looks down demurely, avoiding the adoring gaze of a gentleman sitting in profile. This man is a self-portrait of the artist. Lawless was a successful draughtsman and book illustrator, whose known oil paintings are very small in number. His meticulous technique was influenced by contemporary French academic painting, especially the highly polished style of Ernest Meisonnier. Unfortunately, Lawless's short life was plagued by illness and he died from consumption at the age of twenty-seven.

M	T	W	T	F	S	S
31	1	2	3	4	5	6
7	8	9	10	11	12	13
14	15	16	17	18	19	20
21	22	23	24	25	26	27
28	29	30	31	1	2	3

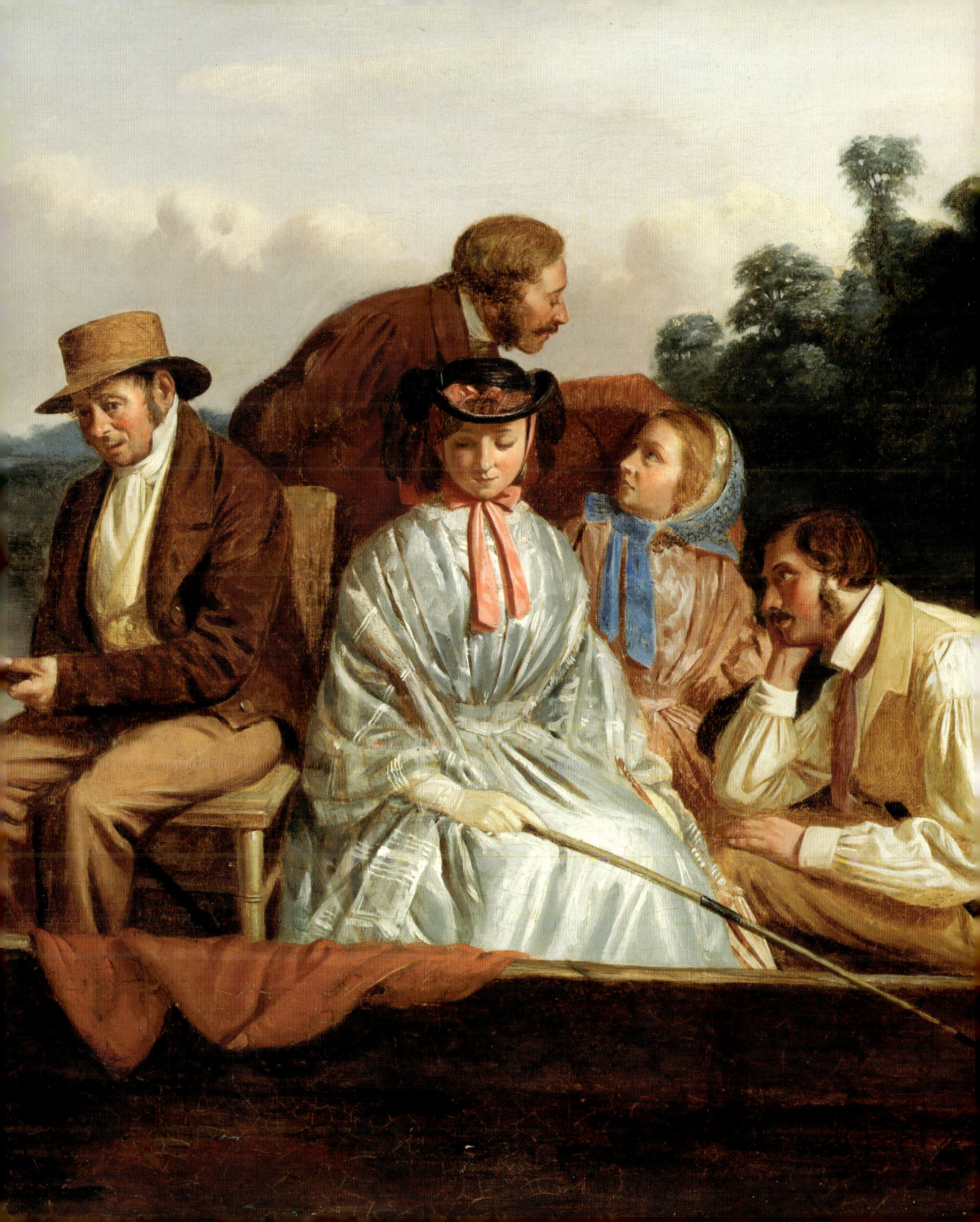

May • Bealtaine
Week 21 • Seachtain 21

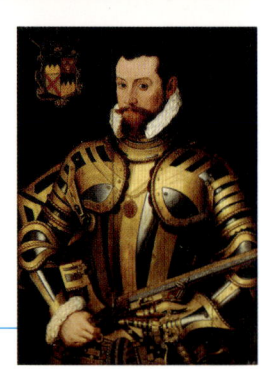

21 Monday • Luan

22 Tuesday • Máirt

23 Wednesday • Céadaoin

24 Thursday • Déardaoin

25 Friday • Aoine

26 Saturday • Satharn

27 Sunday • Domhnach

Attributed to Steven van der Meulen, *Portrait of Thomas Butler, 10th Earl of Ormond (1532–1614),* **1560s**

This is one of the earliest portraits of an Irish noble and depicts Thomas Butler wearing a gilt suit of cavalry armour and holding a wheel lock pistol. Known as the 'Black Earl' due to his dark complexion, Butler was son and heir of the 9th Earl of Ormond. He was brought to the English Court at fourteen and became a supporter of the Crown. He returned to Ireland to fight the Scots, was a Privy Councillor to both Queen Mary Tudor and Queen Elizabeth I and became Lord Treasurer of Ireland.

M	T	W	T	F	S	S
31	1	2	3	4	5	6
7	8	9	10	11	12	13
14	15	16	17	18	19	20
21	22	23	24	25	26	27
28	29	30	31	1	2	3

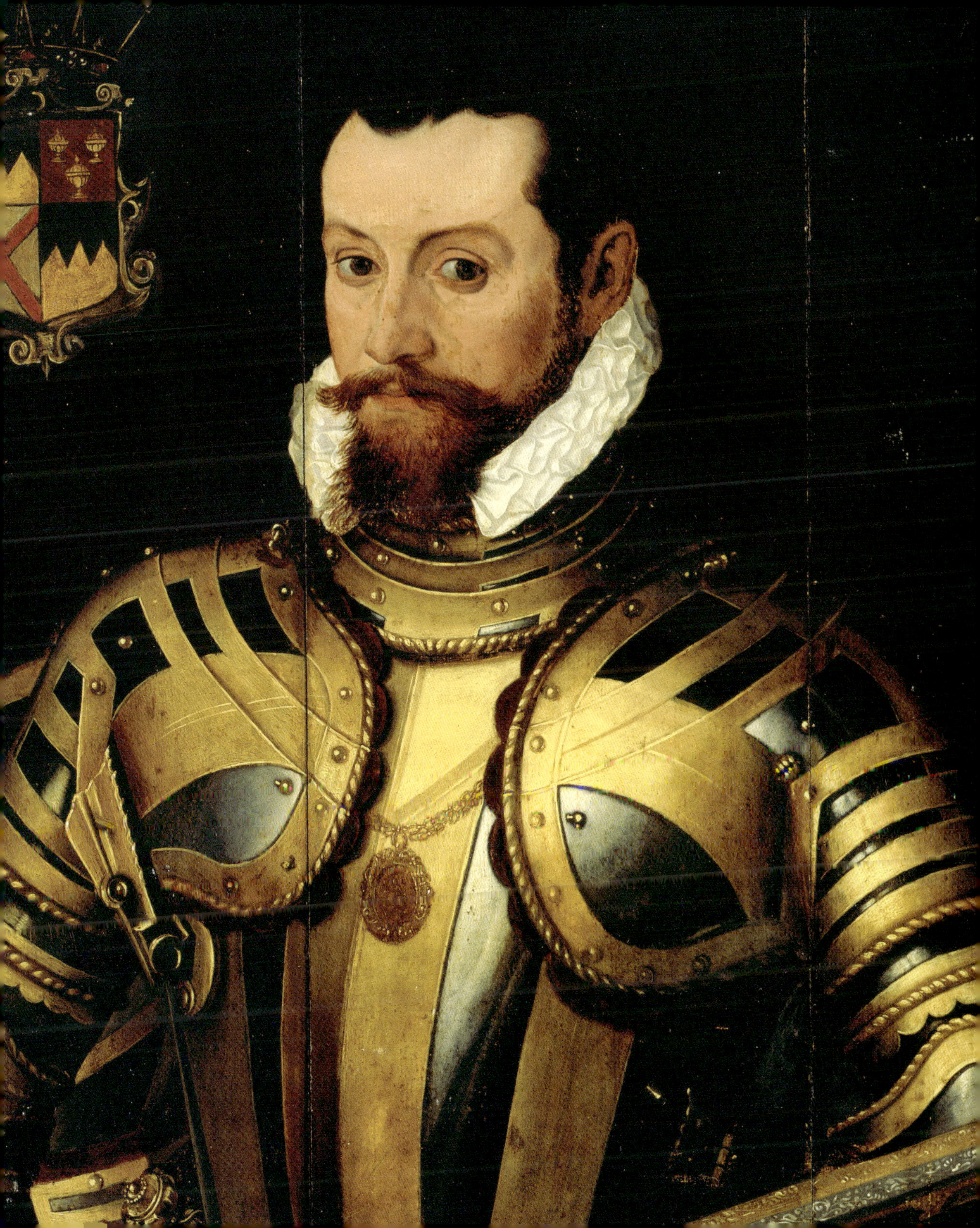

May • Bealtaine
Week 22 • Seachtain 22

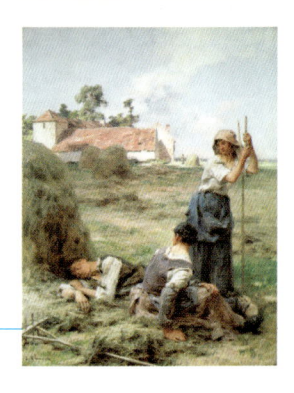

28 Monday • Luan

29 Tuesday • Máirt

30 Wednesday • Céadaoin

31 Thursday • Déardaoin

1 Friday • Aoine   **June • Meitheamh**

2 Saturday • Satharn

3 Sunday • Domhnach

Léon-Augustin Lhermitte, *Harvesters at Rest,* **1888**

The French Realist painter Léon Lhermitte specialised in idealised images of peasants at work. This scene, like many of his depictions of rural life, was painted on a large scale that lends an air of gravitas to the rustic figures and their occupations. Although he has used a light palette and sketchy brushwork, Lhermitte's composition is structured according to formal academic conventions. The painting is based on a drawing the artist made in his native village of Mont-Saint-Père in Picardy in 1886.

M	T	W	T	F	S	S
31	1	2	3	4	5	6
7	8	9	10	11	12	13
14	15	16	17	18	19	20
21	22	23	24	25	26	27
28	29	30	31	1	2	3

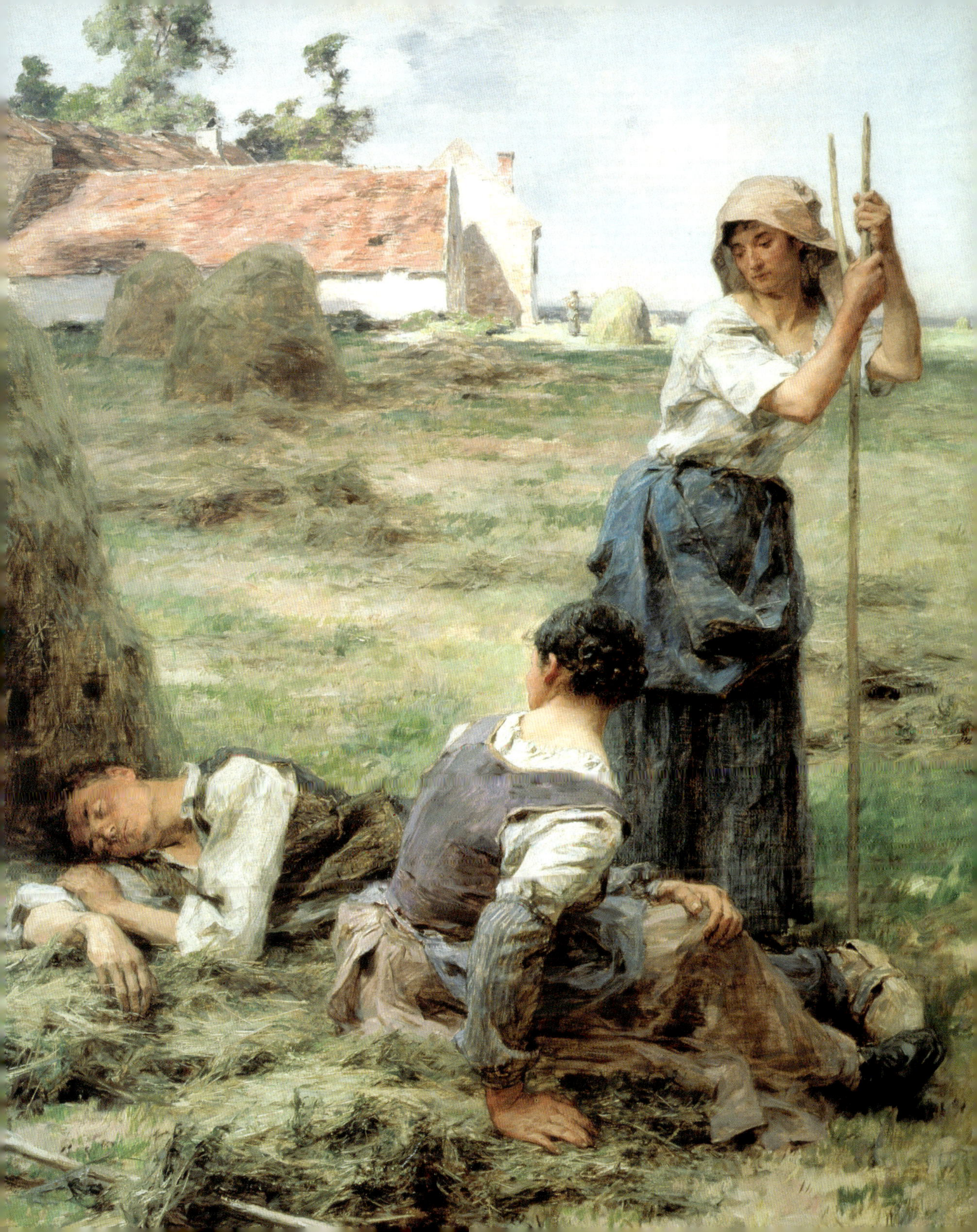

June · Meitheamh
Week 23 · Seachtain 23

4 Monday · Luan
Bank holiday (RoI and UK)

5 Tuesday · Máirt
Bank holiday (UK)

6 Wednesday · Céadaoin

7 Thursday · Déardaoin

8 Friday · Aoine

9 Saturday · Satharn

10 Sunday · Domhnach

Thomas Roberts, *A View of Ballyshannon, County Donegal,* **1770**

Roberts painted along Upper and Lower Lough Erne and this view looks westwards, across an eel weir and a fourteen-arch bridge to the island of Inis Saimer and out to the Atlantic. The wealthier district of Ballyshannon, known as The Rock, is on the right, while the poorer area, The Purt, is on the left. Roberts's powers of observation are evident in his accurate recording of natural and architectural features. Roberts was one of the most talented Irish painters of the 18th century, but he died at the age of twenty-eight.

M	T	W	T	F	S	S
28	29	30	31	1	2	3
4	5	6	7	8	9	10
11	12	13	14	15	16	17
18	19	20	21	22	23	24
25	26	27	28	29	30	1

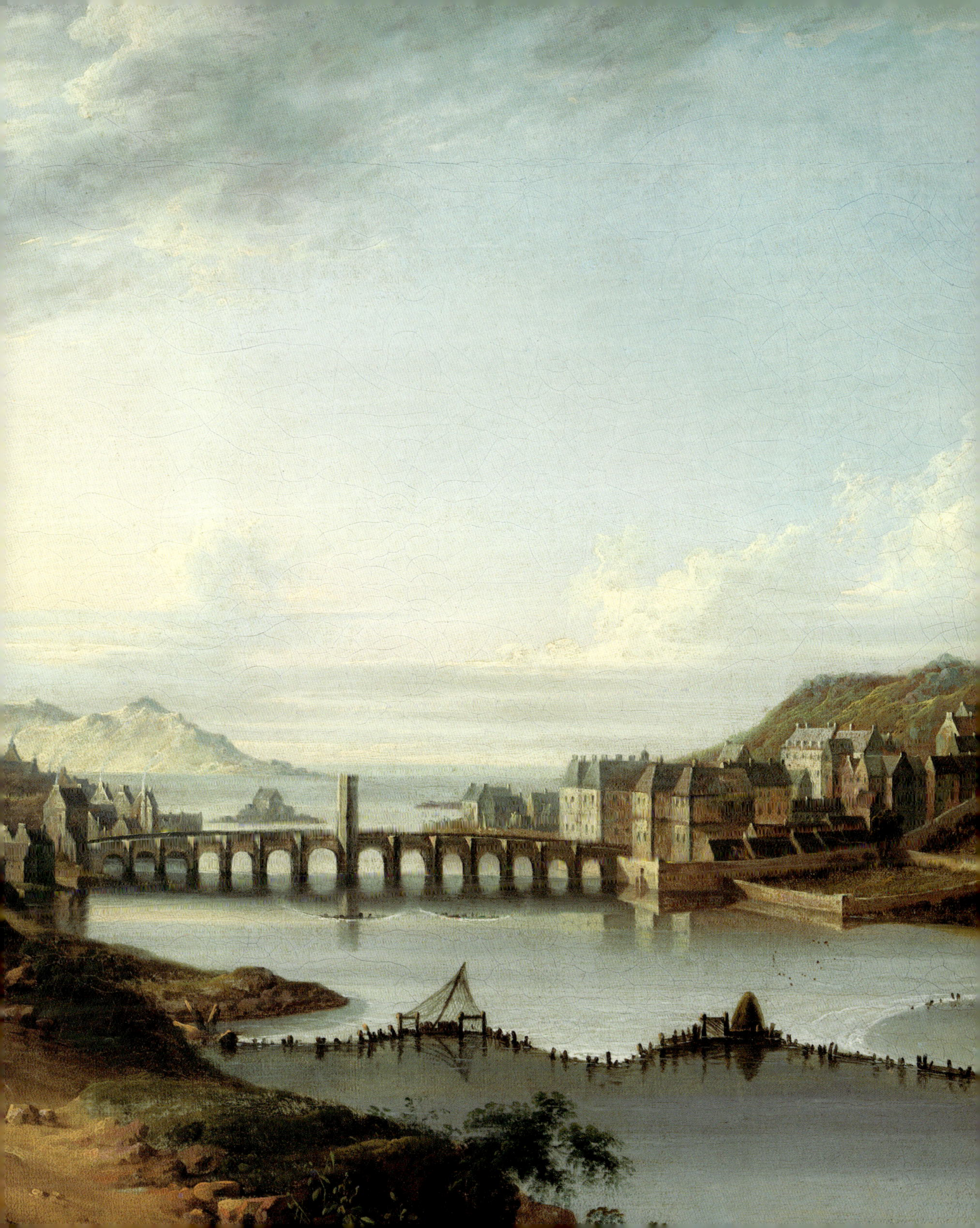

June • Meitheamh
Week 24 • Seachtain 24

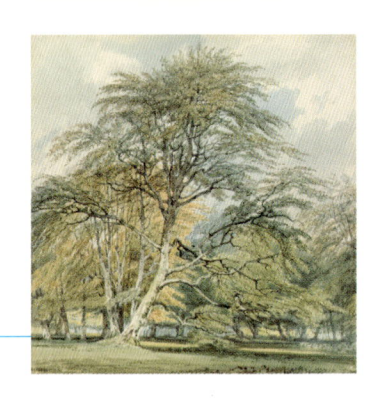

11 Monday • Luan

12 Tuesday • Máirt

13 Wednesday • Céadaoin

14 Thursday • Déardaoin

15 Friday • Aoine

16 Saturday • Satharn

17 Sunday • Domhnach

Joseph Mallord William Turner, *Beech Trees at Norbury Park, Surrey,* **c.1797**

In 1797, the young Turner visited Norbury Park in Surrey, home of the sculptor, collector and patron of the arts William Locke, who commissioned him to paint a view of the fernhouse at his demesne. While working there, Turner made detailed studies of the great beech trees on the estate. In this watercolour he captures their graceful branches and delicate foliage in a light, feathery technique. This reveals the sensitivity of brushwork that begins to appear in Turner's work around this date, when his confidence in depicting nature was growing.

M	T	W	T	F	S	S
28	29	30	31	1	2	3
4	5	6	7	8	9	10
11	12	13	14	15	16	17
18	19	20	21	22	23	24
25	26	27	28	29	30	1

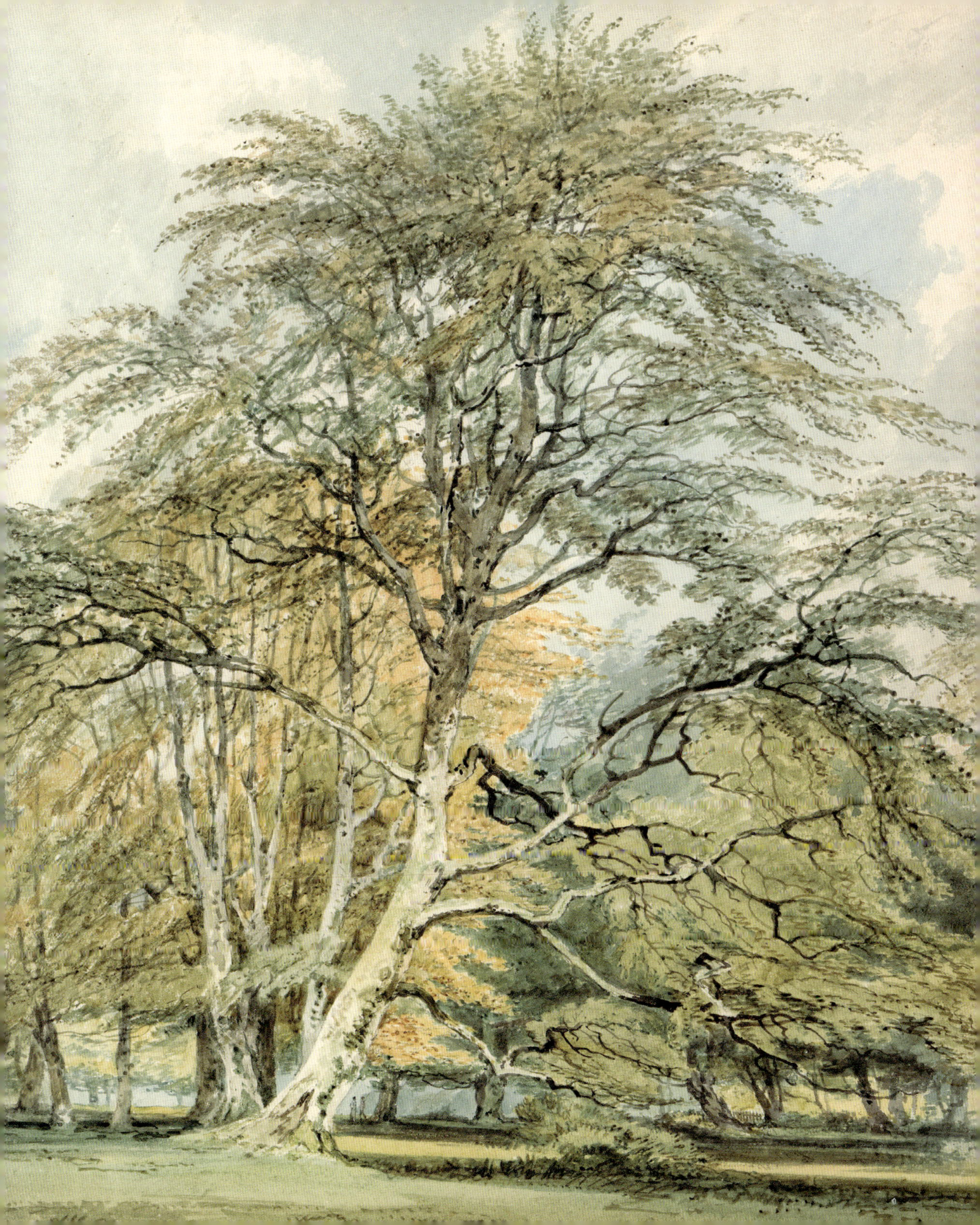

June • Meitheamh
Week 25 • Seachtain 25

18 Monday • Luan

19 Tuesday • Máirt

20 Wednesday • Céadaoin

21 Thursday • Déardaoin

22 Friday • Aoine

23 Saturday • Satharn

24 Sunday • Domhnach

Sarah Henrietta Purser, *A Lady Holding a Doll's Rattle,* **1885**

The Irish woman holding a rattle, Mary Maud de la Poer Beresford, was the daughter of Colonel Marcus de la Poer Beresford and the wife of Julian Sturgis. Sarah Purser spent the late summer of 1885 with Mary and Julian in Surrey, producing seven pictures of them. An inscription at the bottom of this canvas indicates that Purser dedicated the work to Julian Sturgis. It is a lively sketch, painted with a confidence and economy that recalls Purser's time in Paris and suggests the influence of Impressionism.

M	T	W	T	F	S	S
28	29	30	31	1	2	3
4	5	6	7	8	9	10
11	12	13	14	15	16	17
18	19	20	21	22	23	24
25	26	27	28	29	30	1

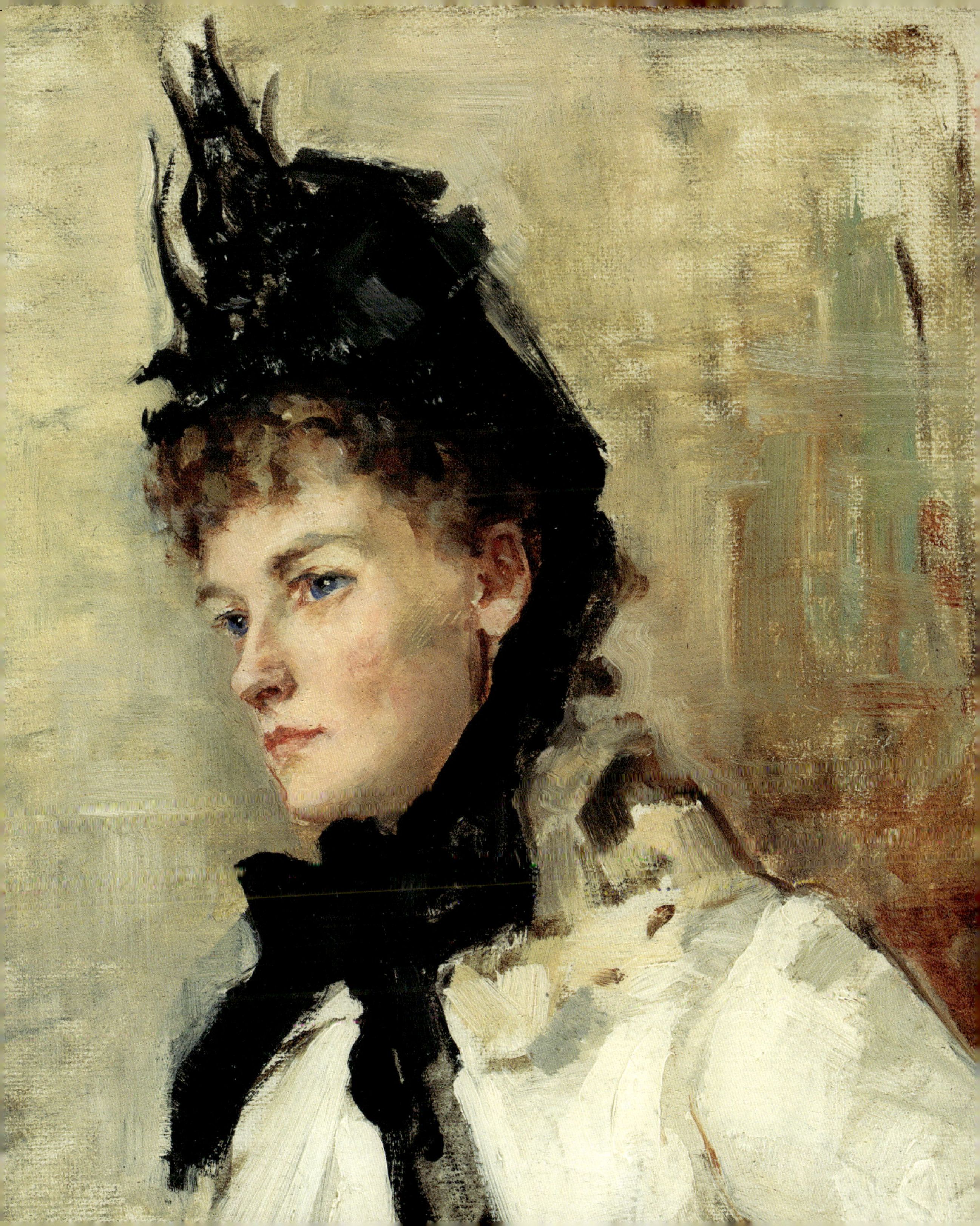

June • Meitheamh
Week 26 • Seachtain 26

25 Monday • Luan

26 Tuesday • Máirt

27 Wednesday • Céadaoin

28 Thursday • Déardaoin

29 Friday • Aoine

30 Saturday • Satharn

1 Sunday • Domhnach   July • Iúil

John Luke, *Shaw's Bridge,* **c.1934**

This print is a good example of John Luke's highly decorative style, which contributes to the dreamlike atmosphere of this landscape, despite the precise recording of figures, dogs and swans. The high quality of the print and his use of Japanese paper are characteristic of the artist's few known linocuts. He often restricted himself to black and white when working in the print medium. Luke worked as a painter, printmaker and art teacher in Belfast, where he exhibited this linocut in Locksley Hall in 1934.

M	T	W	T	F	S	S
28	29	30	31	1	2	3
4	5	6	7	8	9	10
11	12	13	14	15	16	17
18	19	20	21	22	23	24
25	26	27	28	29	30	1

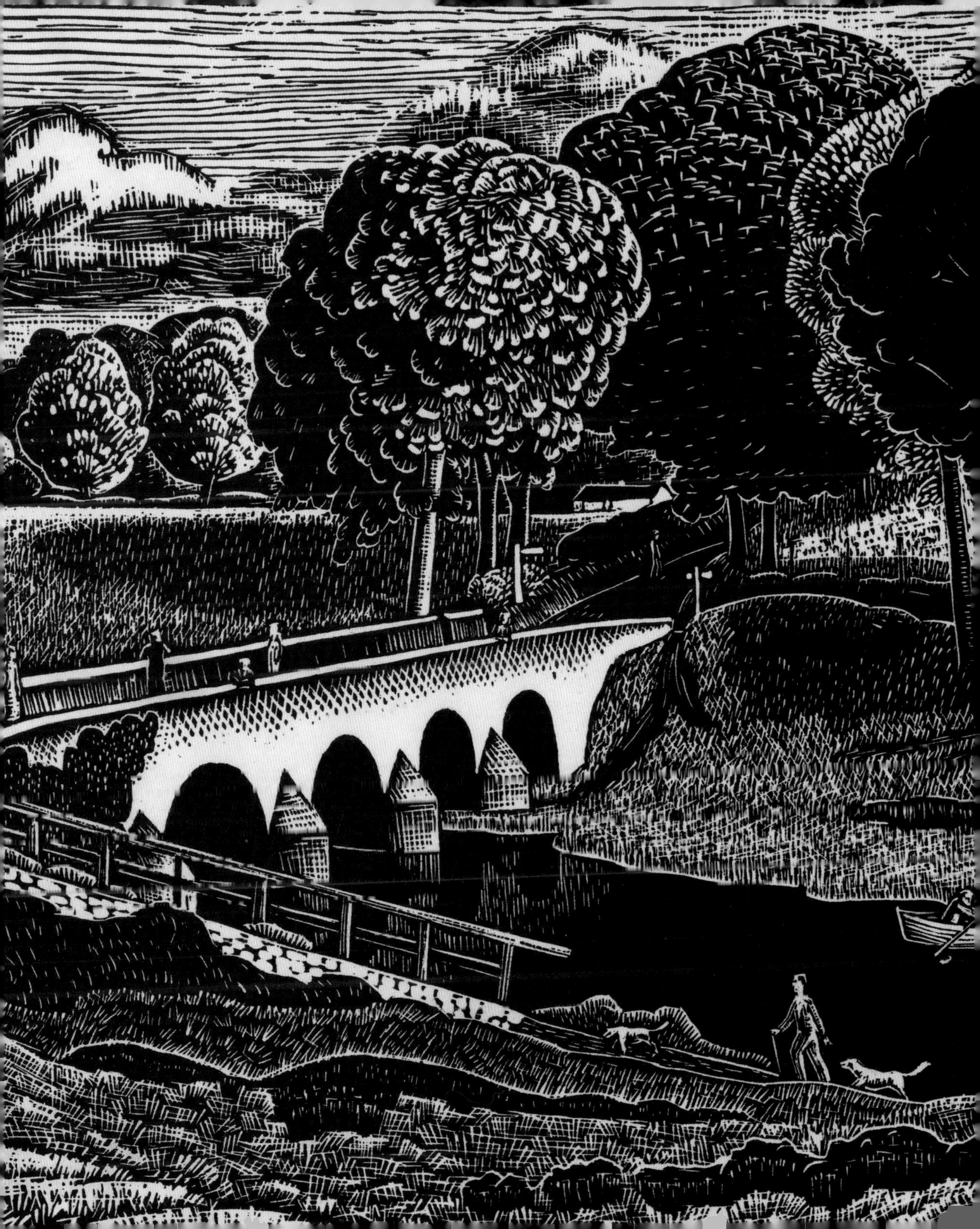

July • Iúil
Week 27 • Seachtain 27

2 Monday • Luan

3 Tuesday • Máirt

4 Wednesday • Céadaoin

5 Thursday • Déardaoin

6 Friday • Aoine

7 Saturday • Satharn

8 Sunday • Domhnach

Edwin Hayes, *An Emigrant Ship, Dublin Bay, Sunset,* **1853**

This painting addresses the subject of mass emigration in the years immediately following the Great Famine. A sailing ship at anchor at the mouth of the River Liffey waits for emigrants to board. Conditions on board those ships bound for America and Australia were often appalling and many passengers did not survive the journey. The dramatic sunset in this painting, however, might be said to herald a safe journey and kinder future for those travelling.

M	T	W	T	F	S	S
25	26	27	28	29	30	1
2	3	4	5	6	7	8
9	10	11	12	13	14	15
16	17	18	19	20	21	22
23	24	25	26	27	28	29
30	31	1	2	3	4	5

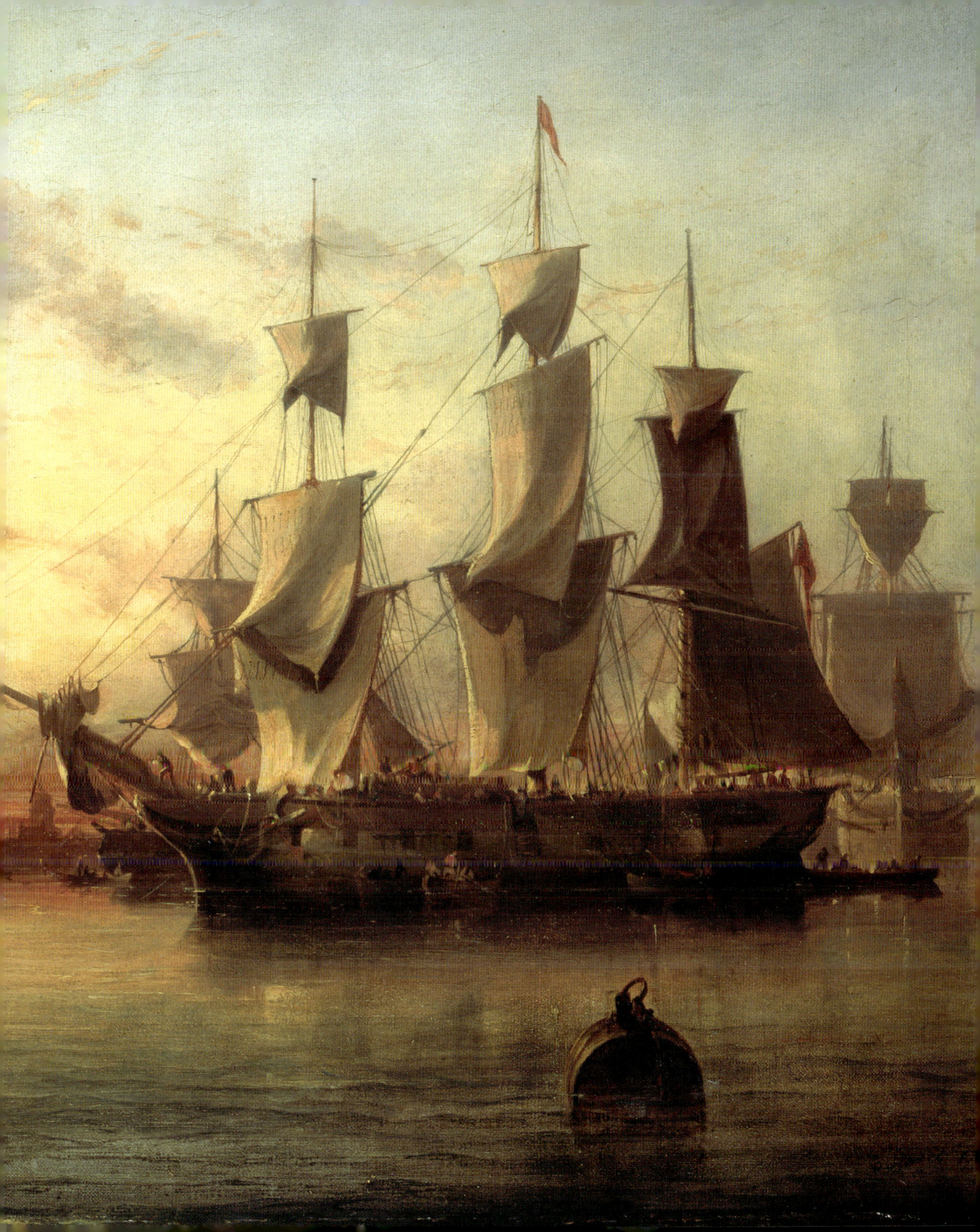

July • Iúil
Week 28 • Seachtain 28

9 Monday • Luan

10 Tuesday • Máirt

11 Wednesday • Céadaoin

12 Thursday • Déardaoin
Bank holiday (NI)

13 Friday • Aoine

14 Saturday • Satharn

15 Sunday • Domhnach

Harry Andersson, *Aladdin,* **1923**

Aladdin is one of the most famous tales in *The Book of One Thousand and One Nights (Arabian Nights).* The original story was a Middle-Eastern folk tale and this is the setting chosen by Andersson for his print. In the background, servants silhouetted in black against white carry goods towards Aladdin's palace. In the foreground, characters in Eastern dress are highlighted in white against black: Aladdin on horseback, the sorcerer, servants, musicians and the djinni with his lamp. The woodcut technique is ideal for producing such a dramatic, graphic image.

M	T	W	T	F	S	S
25	26	27	28	29	30	1
2	3	4	5	6	7	8
9	10	11	12	13	14	15
16	17	18	19	20	21	22
23	24	25	26	27	28	29
30	31	1	2	3	4	5

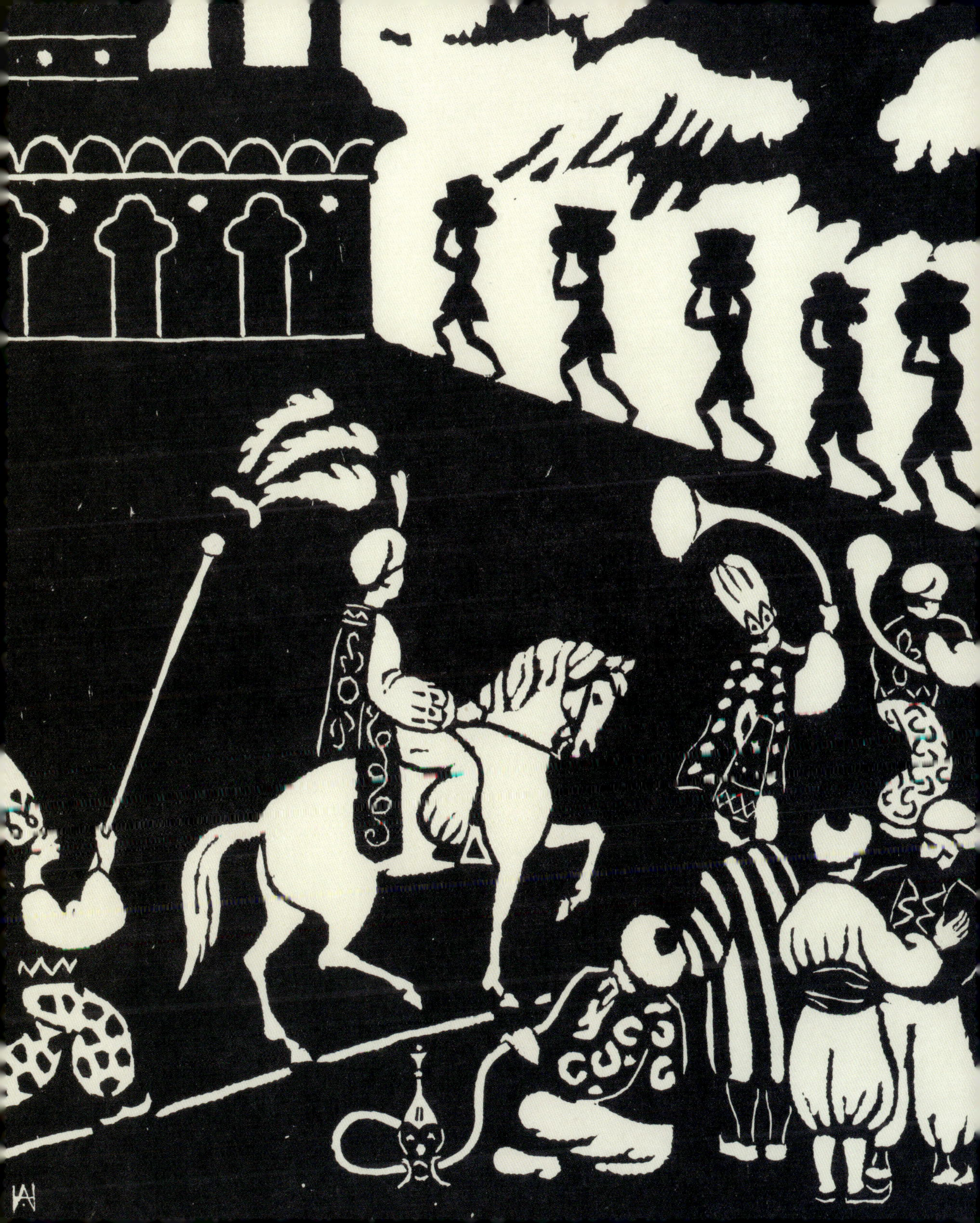

July • Iúil
Week 29 • Seachtain 29

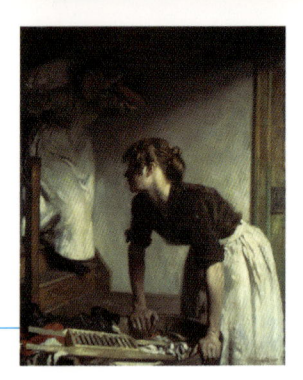

16 Monday • Luan

17 Tuesday • Máirt

18 Wednesday • Céadaoin

19 Thursday • Déardaoin

20 Friday • Aoine

21 Saturday • Satharn

22 Sunday • Domhnach

William Orpen, *The Wash House,* **1905**

The model for this painting was Lottie Stafford, a cockney washerwoman who lived and worked in Paradise Walk, a slum neighbourhood in Chelsea, East London. She became one of Orpen's favourite models. Here she is captured pausing momentarily to look up from her washboard at a woman descending the stairs carrying laundry. Lottie's face is caught in profile while light falls on her neck, a feature that particularly appealed to Orpen. He records a washerwoman's arduous toil, but softens the image through the delicacy of his modelling.

M	T	W	T	F	S	S
25	26	27	28	29	30	1
2	3	4	5	6	7	8
9	10	11	12	13	14	15
16	17	18	19	20	21	22
23	24	25	26	27	28	29
30	31	1	2	3	4	5

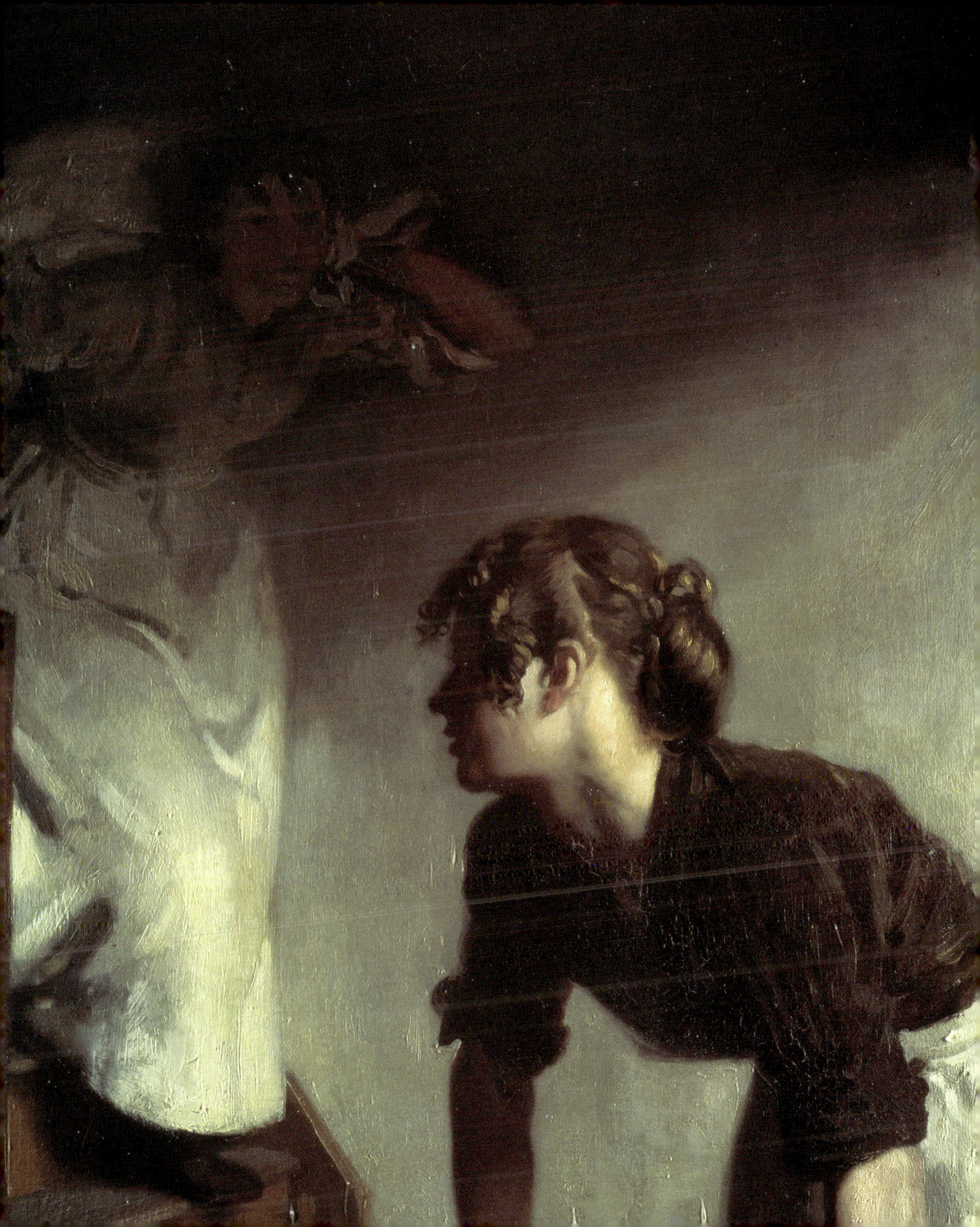

July • Iúil
Week 30 • Seachtain 30

23 Monday • Luan

24 Tuesday • Máirt

25 Wednesday • Céadaoin

26 Thursday • Déardaoin

27 Friday • Aoine

28 Saturday • Satharn

29 Sunday • Domhnach

Paul Henry, *Launching the Curragh,* **1910–1911**

The bent posture of these five fishermen communicates their effort in dragging their boat towards the water. The curragh, made of wickerwork and hide, was ideally suited to both shallow waters and rough seas. Henry was inspired by the rugged character of Achill's inhabitants, for whom fishing was a necessary but also dangerous industry. The turbulent sea reinforces the harsh reality and uncertainty of the life of an island fisherman.

M	T	W	T	F	S	S
25	26	27	28	29	30	1
2	3	4	5	6	7	8
9	10	11	12	13	14	15
16	17	18	19	20	21	22
23	24	25	26	27	28	29
30	31	1	2	3	4	5

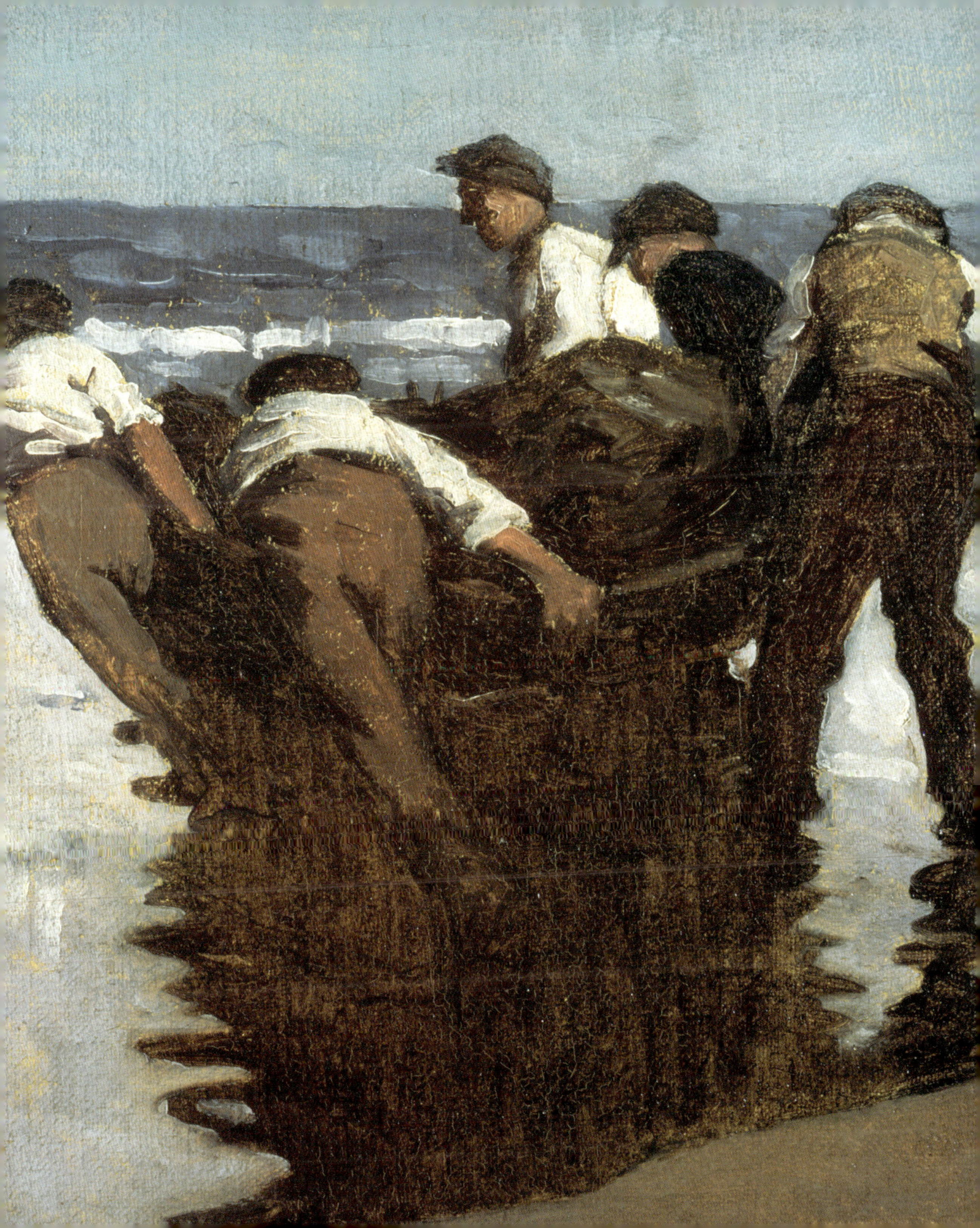

July • Iúil
Week 31 • Seachtain 31

30 Monday • Luan

31 Tuesday • Máirt

1 Wednesday • Céadaoin   August • Lúnasa

2 Thursday • Déardaoin

3 Friday • Aoine

4 Saturday • Satharn

5 Sunday • Domhnach

Robert Ponsonby Staples, *Ireland's Eye from Howth,* **1899**

Ponsonby Staples has combined graphite, pastel, chalk and watercolour to create a fresh and spontaneous landscape, which was more than likely painted rapidly *en plein air* (in the open air). Beyond a haystack, the Martello tower to the left of Ireland's Eye can be detected, balanced on the right by the huge, blue-tinged, freestanding rock known as 'the Stack'. Lambay Island is visible in the distance. The openness of the North Dublin coastline is conveyed in this view which, unusually for the artist's work, is devoid of human figures.

M	T	W	T	F	S	S
25	26	27	28	29	30	1
2	3	4	5	6	7	8
9	10	11	12	13	14	15
16	17	18	19	20	21	22
23	24	25	26	27	28	29
30	31	1	2	3	4	5

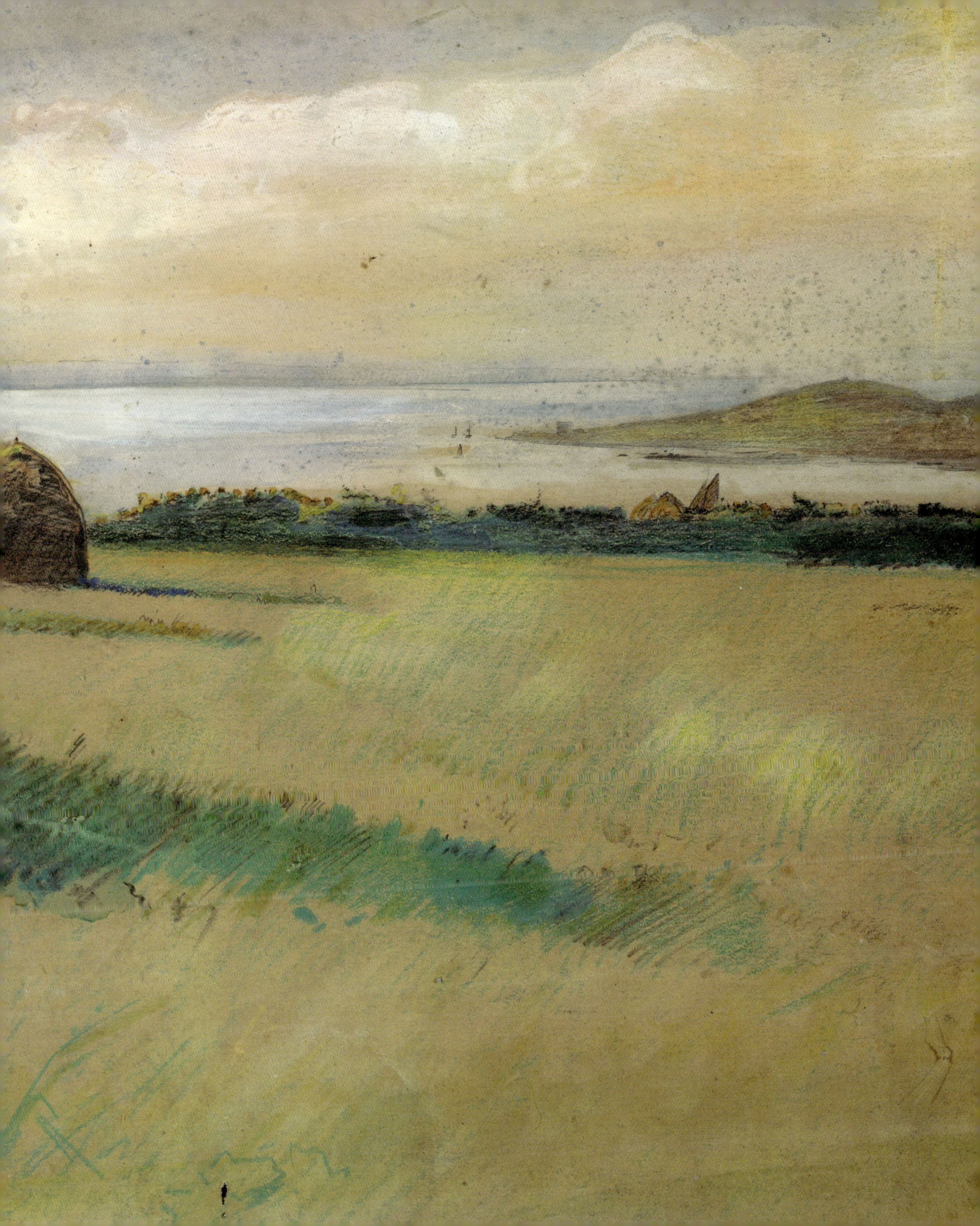

August · Lúnasa
Week 32 · Seachtain 32

6 Monday · Luan
Bank holiday (RoI and Scotland)

7 Tuesday · Máirt

8 Wednesday · Céadaoin

9 Thursday · Déardaoin

10 Friday · Aoine

11 Saturday · Satharn

12 Sunday · Domhnach

Matthew James Lawless, *A Sick Call,* **1863**

A grave-looking priest, accompanied by a similarly sombre party, crosses a river to administer the Last Rites to a dying person. The picture, one of small number of recognised works by the artist, reflects Lawless's admiration for earlier 19th-century French painting, but also his knowledge of Dutch 17th-century art, while the architectural detail and setting were inspired by his travels in northern Europe and, perhaps, a drawing of Prague that he had admired. The subject itself is best understood in the context of Lawless's own persistent ill health.

M	T	W	T	F	S	S
30	31	1	2	3	4	5
6	7	8	9	10	11	12
13	14	15	16	17	18	19
20	21	22	23	24	25	26
27	28	29	30	31	1	2

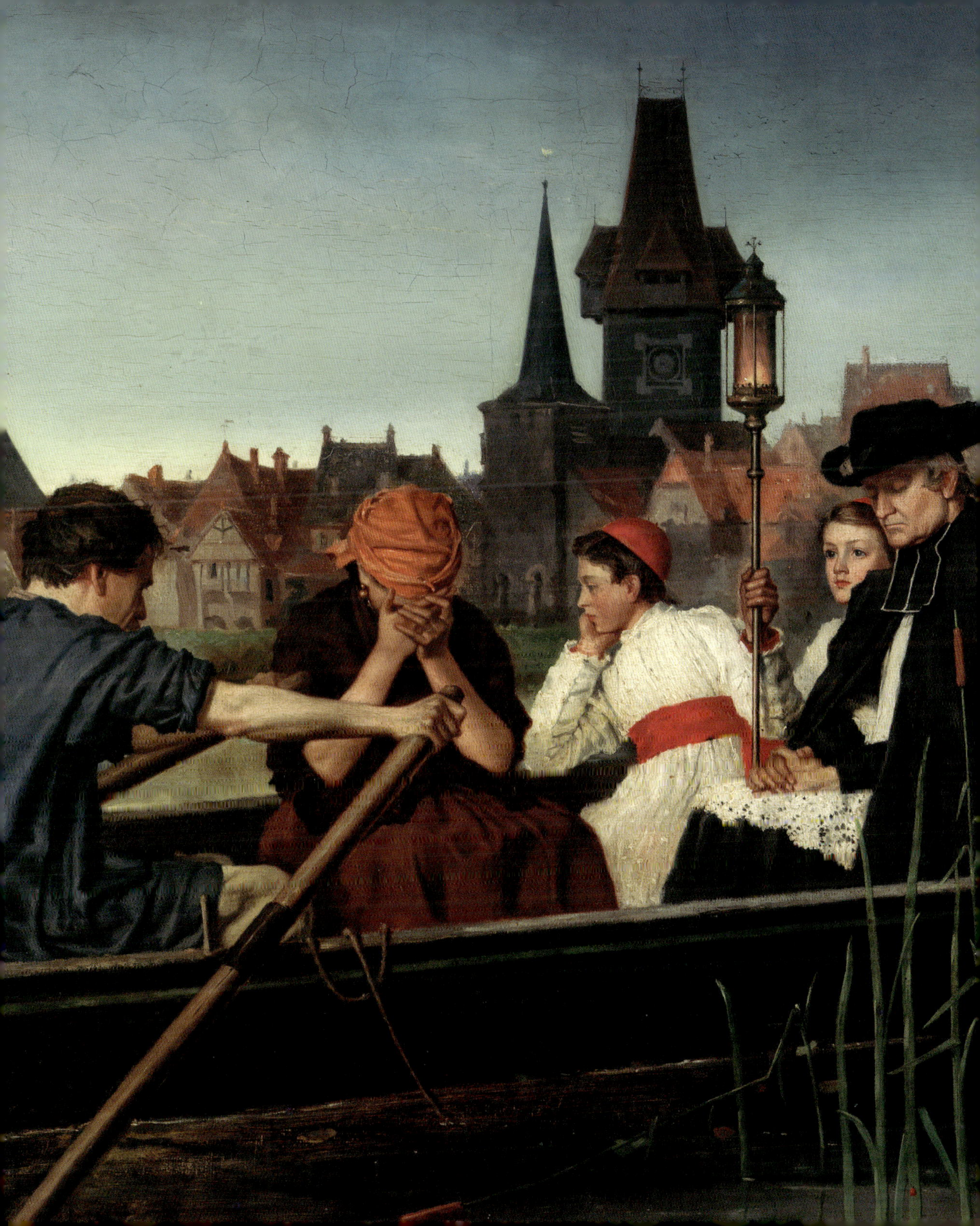

August • Lúnasa
Week 33 • Seachtain 33

13 Monday • Luan

14 Tuesday • Máirt

15 Wednesday • Céadaoin

16 Thursday • Déardaoin

17 Friday • Aoine

18 Saturday • Satharn

19 Sunday • Domhnach

Guercino, *The Virgin and Child (for the Madonna del Carmine Presenting a Scapular to a Carmelite, in Cento's Pinacoteca Civica),* **c.1615**

This is a preparatory drawing for an altarpiece now in the Pinacoteca Civica at Cento, Guercino's home town in northern Italy. The Madonna del Carmine (Our Lady of Mount Carmel) is shown with the Christ Child presenting a scapular to the Carmelite monk Saint Albert. A scapular was originally a type of apron worn by monks consisting of pieces of cloth worn front and back, joined by straps over the shoulders. It forms part of the habit of some religious orders, including the Carmelites, for whom it remains a sign of Mary's motherly protection.

M	T	W	T	F	S	S
30	31	1	2	3	4	5
6	7	8	9	10	11	12
13	14	15	16	17	18	19
20	21	22	23	24	25	26
27	28	29	30	31	1	2

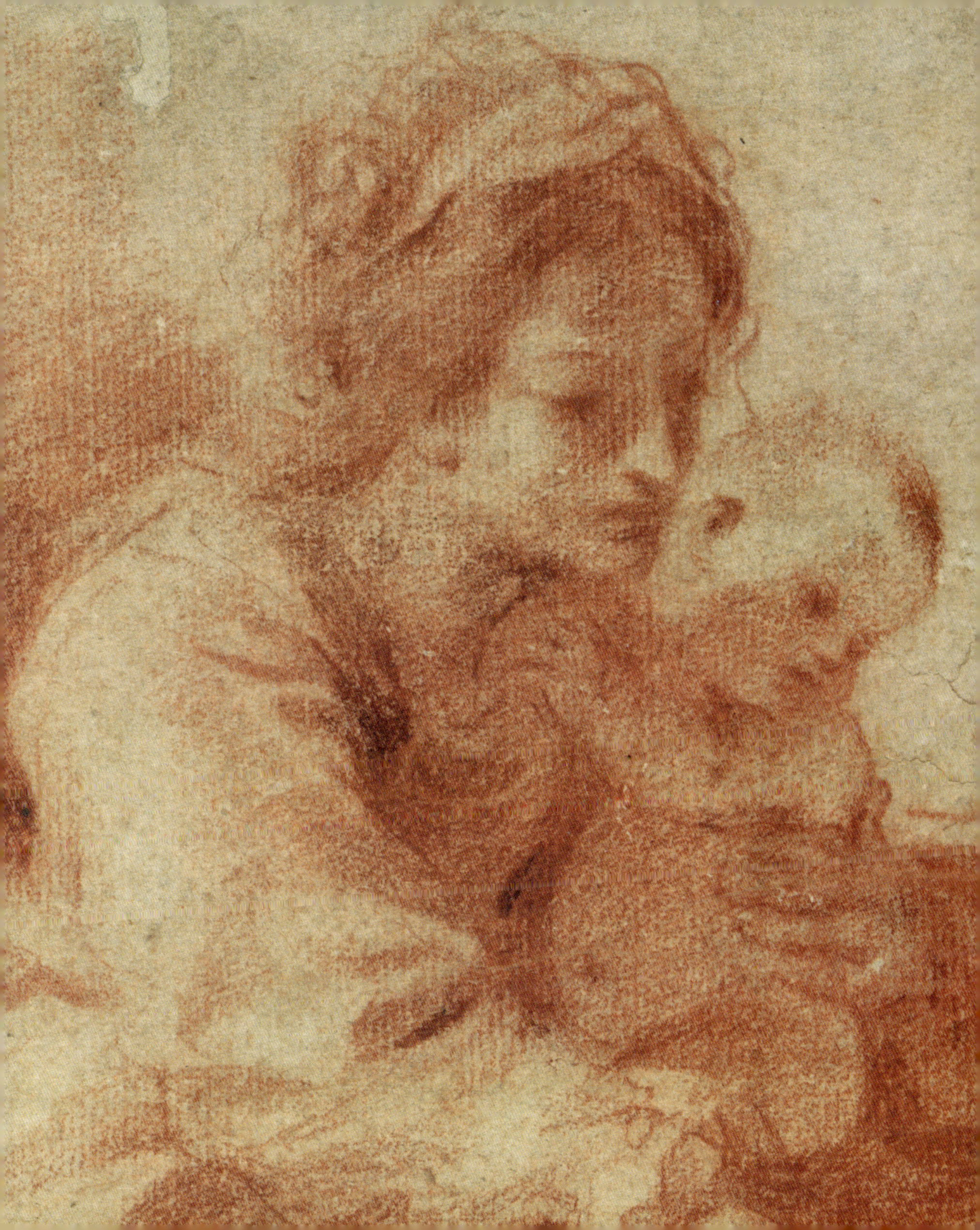

August • Lúnasa
Week 34 • Seachtain 34

20 Monday • Luan

21 Tuesday • Máirt

22 Wednesday • Céadaoin

23 Thursday • Déardaoin

24 Friday • Aoine

25 Saturday • Satharn

26 Sunday • Domhnach

Thomas Hickey, *Portrait of two Children,* **1769**

In this charming painting, one girl holds an orange while the other carries a small basket. Their simple white gowns and coloured sashes were typical of a period when children were dressed in miniature versions of adult clothing. Although there is no record of Hickey having children of his own by this date, the character of the picture calls to mind Gainsborough's painting of his two daughters chasing a butterfly (1756, National Gallery London). Both works are reflections of the brevity of childhood and the innocence of youth, but are not overly sentimental.

M	T	W	T	F	S	S
30	31	1	2	3	4	5
6	7	8	9	10	11	12
13	14	15	16	17	18	19
20	21	22	23	24	25	26
27	28	29	30	31	1	2

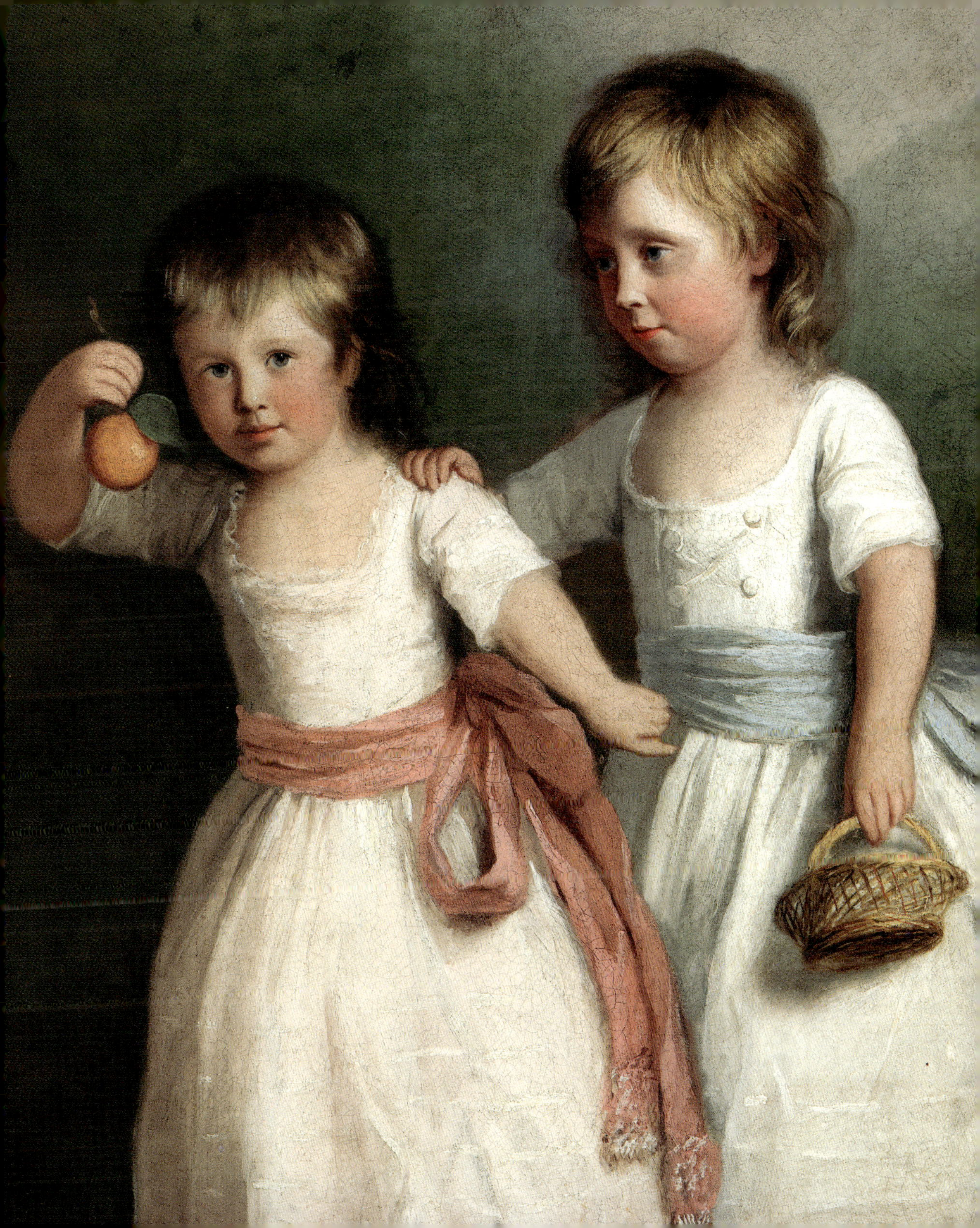

August • Lúnasa
Week 35 • Seachtain 35

27 Monday • Luan
Bank holiday (UK)

28 Tuesday • Máirt

29 Wednesday • Céadaoin

30 Thursday • Déardaoin

31 Friday • Aoine

1 Saturday • Satharn   September • Meán Fómhair

2 Sunday • Domhnach

Aloysius O'Kelly, *Preparing for Winter,* 1880s

O'Kelly was one of many artists who travelled to Brittany in the late 19th century and painted the costumes, customs and activities of the Breton people. His experience in France informed his later work elsewhere. In this picture, painted in Kent in southeast England, O'Kelly records everyday activity and local detail with familiar accuracy. The elderly man's bowler hat and whiskers are typical of the region, while the billhook with which he works, used for cutting branches, saplings, hedging and snedding, was known locally as a Kentish brishing hook.

M	T	W	T	F	S	S
30	31	1	2	3	4	5
6	7	8	9	10	11	12
13	14	15	16	17	18	19
20	21	22	23	24	25	26
27	28	29	30	31	1	2

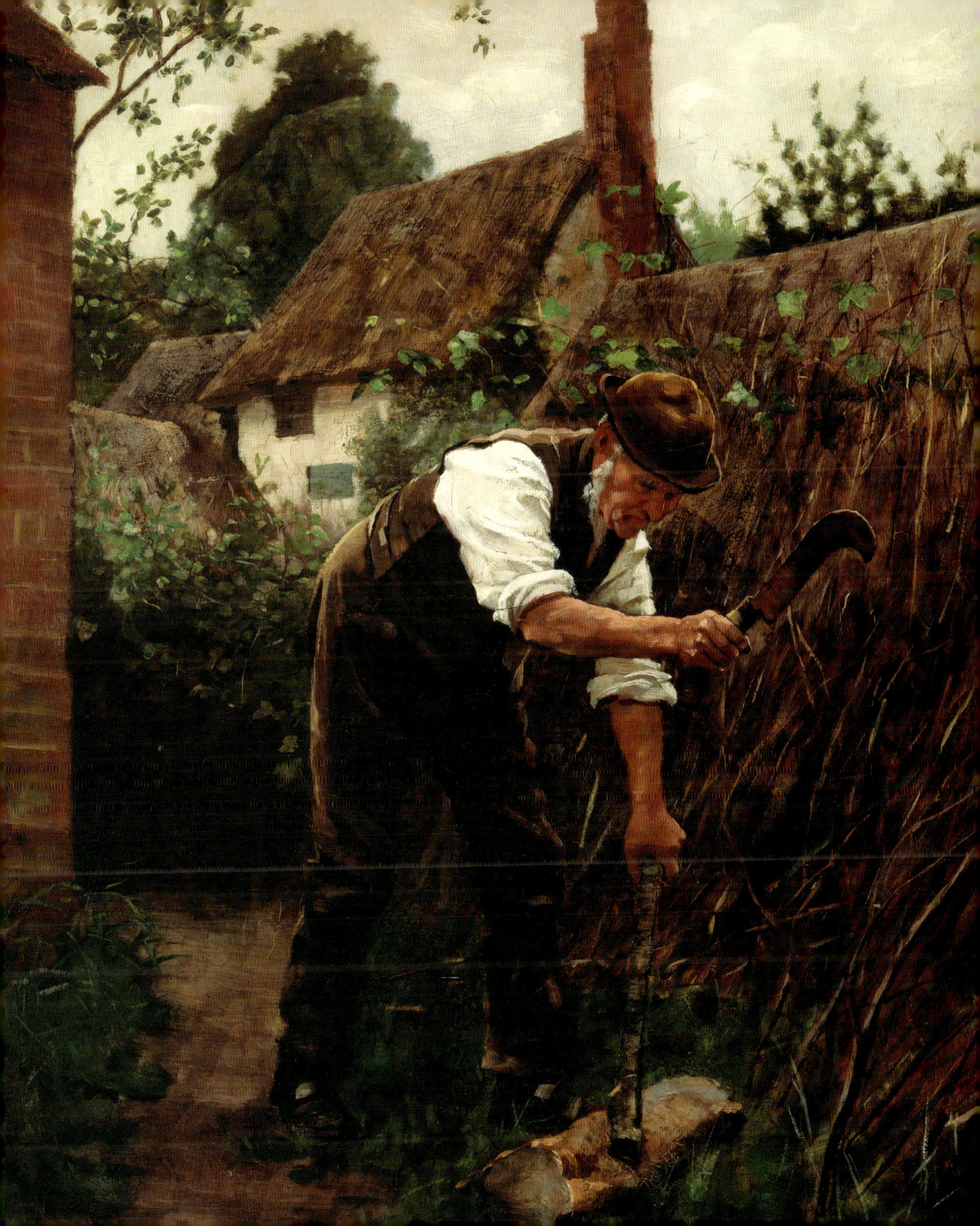

September · Meán Fómhair
Week 36 · Seachtain 36

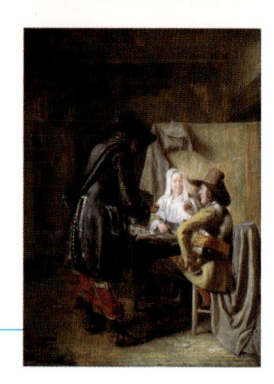

---

3 Monday · Luan

---

4 Tuesday · Máirt

---

5 Wednesday · Céadaoin

---

6 Thursday · Déardaoin

---

7 Friday · Aoine

---

8 Saturday · Satharn

---

9 Sunday · Domhnach

Pieter de Hooch, *Players at Tric-trac,* **c.1652–1655**

Two soldiers and a woman play tric-trac, or backgammon, a game associated in De Hooch's time with idleness and seen as leading to licentiousness and sin. Gambling between the sexes was understood as a preliminary to seduction of women by men, while drinking and smoking were also seen as morally condemnatory. In this scene, one soldier holds a tankard of wine while the other smokes tobacco from a clay pipe. Another used pipe lies discarded on the floor alongside two playing cards, which further emphasise the theme of gambling.

M	T	W	T	F	S	S
27	28	29	30	31	1	2
3	4	5	6	7	8	9
10	11	12	13	14	15	16
17	18	19	20	21	22	23
24	25	26	27	28	29	30

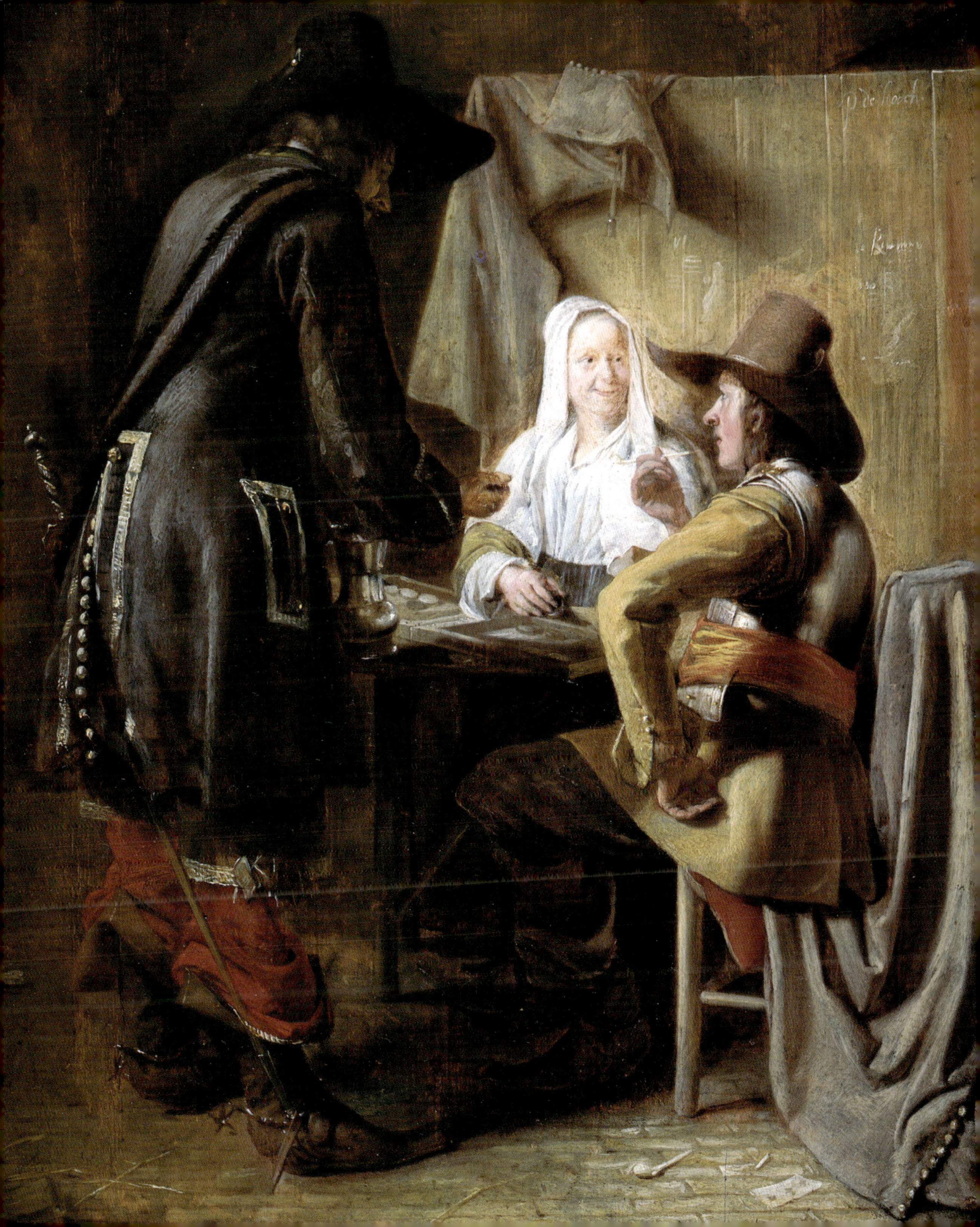
p de hooch

September · Meán Fómhair
Week 37 · Seachtain 37

10 Monday · Luan

11 Tuesday · Máirt

12 Wednesday · Céadaoin

13 Thursday · Déardaoin

14 Friday · Aoine

15 Saturday · Satharn

16 Sunday · Domhnach

Hugh Douglas Hamilton, *Cupid and Psyche,* **c.1792**

This is a preparatory study for Hamilton's oil painting *Cupid and Psyche in the Nuptial Bower,* also in the National Gallery of Ireland, showing that Hamilton spent much time working out the details of his final painting. His choice of subject was probably influenced by contemporary sculptures of Cupid and Psyche by his friend Antonio Canova. Hamilton's figures may be based on a Pompeiian fresco of a faun pulling a nymph towards him, which the artist may have known through contemporary engravings made of the discoveries at Pompeii.

M	T	W	T	F	S	S
27	28	29	30	31	1	2
3	4	5	6	7	8	9
10	11	12	13	14	15	16
17	18	19	20	21	22	23
24	25	26	27	28	29	30

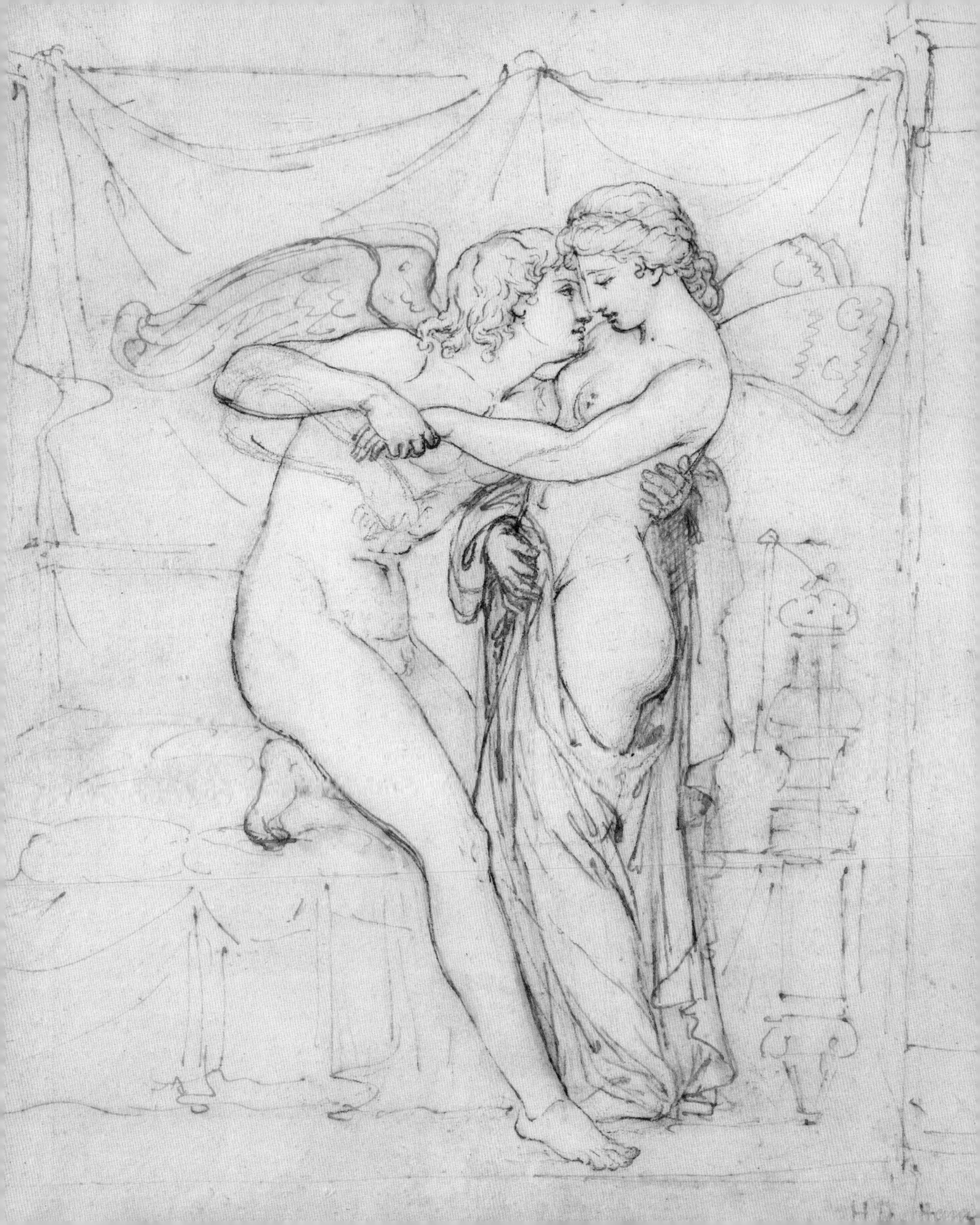

September • Meán Fómhair
Week 38 • Seachtain 38

17 Monday • Luan

18 Tuesday • Máirt

19 Wednesday • Céadaoin

20 Thursday • Déardaoin

21 Friday • Aoine

22 Saturday • Satharn

23 Sunday • Domhnach

James Arthur O'Connor, *A Thunderstorm: The Frightened Wagoner,* **1832**

As a windswept tree strains against a storm, a bolt of lightning cuts through dark clouds and a wagon driver holds his whip aloft and presses his hat to his head. He anxiously surveys the rushing torrent ahead, while his horses, sensing the danger in crossing the fragile bridge, refuse to move forward. The drama of the thunderstorm is conveyed through the movement of trees and water, the contrasting areas of light and shadow and the diminutive status of the wagoner.

M	T	W	T	F	S	S
27	28	29	30	31	1	2
3	4	5	6	7	8	9
10	11	12	13	14	15	16
17	18	19	20	21	22	23
24	25	26	27	28	29	30

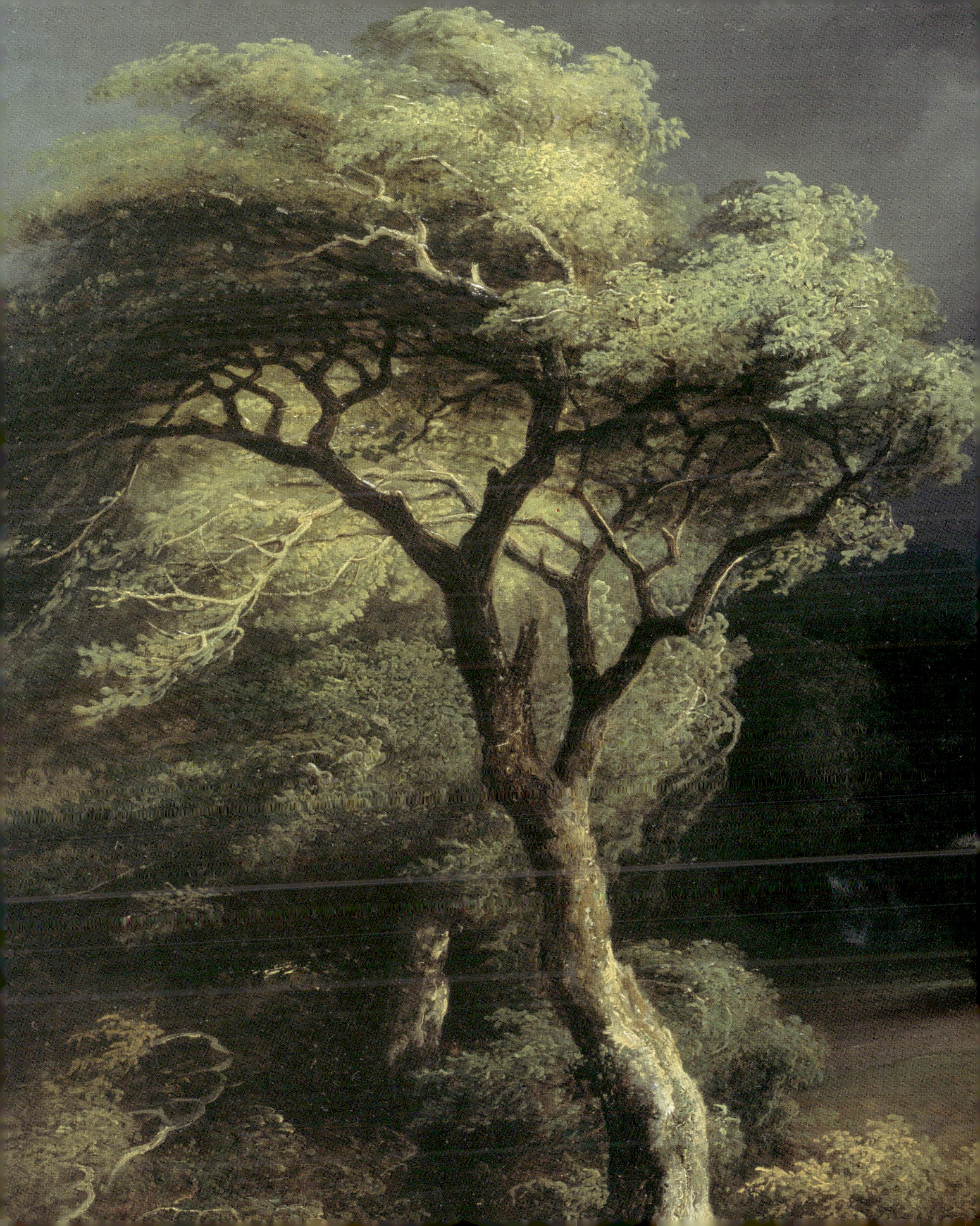

September • Meán Fómhair
Week 39 • Seachtain 39

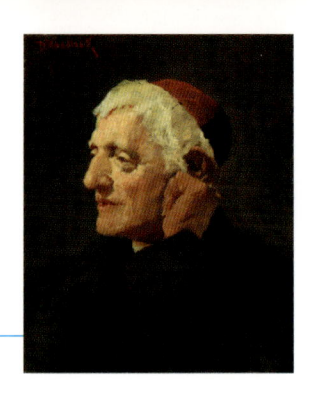

24 Monday • Luan

25 Tuesday • Máirt

26 Wednesday • Céadaoin

27 Thursday • Déardaoin

28 Friday • Aoine

29 Saturday • Satharn

30 Sunday • Domhnach

David Woodlock, *Portrait of Cardinal John Henry Newman (1801–1890),* **c.1888**

Born in London, John Henry Newman attended Trinity College, Oxford, and was ordained in 1824. Concerned by the direction of the Anglican ministry, he took on the leadership of the Oxford Movement, which became the Anglo-Catholic wing of the Church of England. Dramatically, Newman converted to Catholicism in 1845 and became Rector of the newly created Catholic University of Ireland. Newman was a highly influential writer and theologian and was made a Cardinal by Pope Leo XIII and beatified in 2010 by Pope Benedict XVI. The informal pose assumed in Woodlock's portrait was derived from a photograph by William Barraud of 1888.

M	T	W	T	F	S	S
27	28	29	30	31	1	2
3	4	5	6	7	8	9
10	11	12	13	14	15	16
17	18	19	20	21	22	23
24	25	26	27	28	29	30

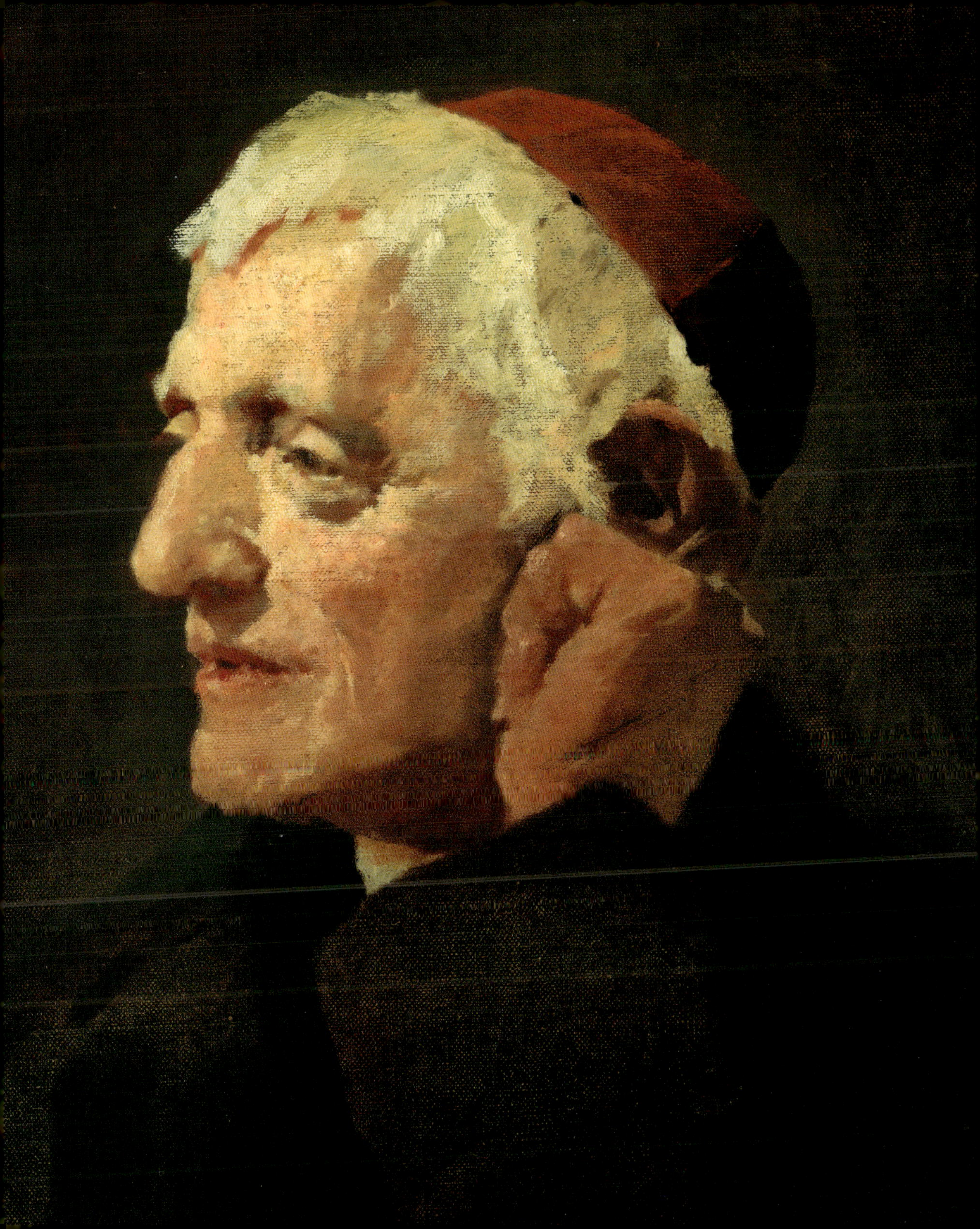

October • Deireadh Fómhair
Week 40 • Seachtain 40

1 Monday • Luan

2 Tuesday • Máirt

3 Wednesday • Céadaoin

4 Thursday • Déardaoin

5 Friday • Aoine

6 Saturday • Satharn

7 Sunday • Domhnach

Robert Ballagh, b.1943, *Portrait of Noel Browne (1915–1997), Politician,* **1985**

Minister for Health Noel Browne's campaign for the eradication of tuberculosis and controversial proposal for free medical care for mothers and children created a Church-State crisis. The Catholic hierarchy claimed it was contrary to Catholic social teaching. Browne refused to abandon his initiative and was forced to resign from his position as Minister in 1951. The cruciform shape of this canvas is often interpreted as an allusion to martyrdom and conflict with the Church. In 1986, Browne's autobiography, *Against the Tide*, written at his home in Connemara, broke Irish publishing records.

M	T	W	T	F	S	S
1	2	3	4	5	6	7
8	9	10	11	12	13	14
15	16	17	18	19	20	21
22	23	24	25	26	27	28
29	30	31	1	2	3	4

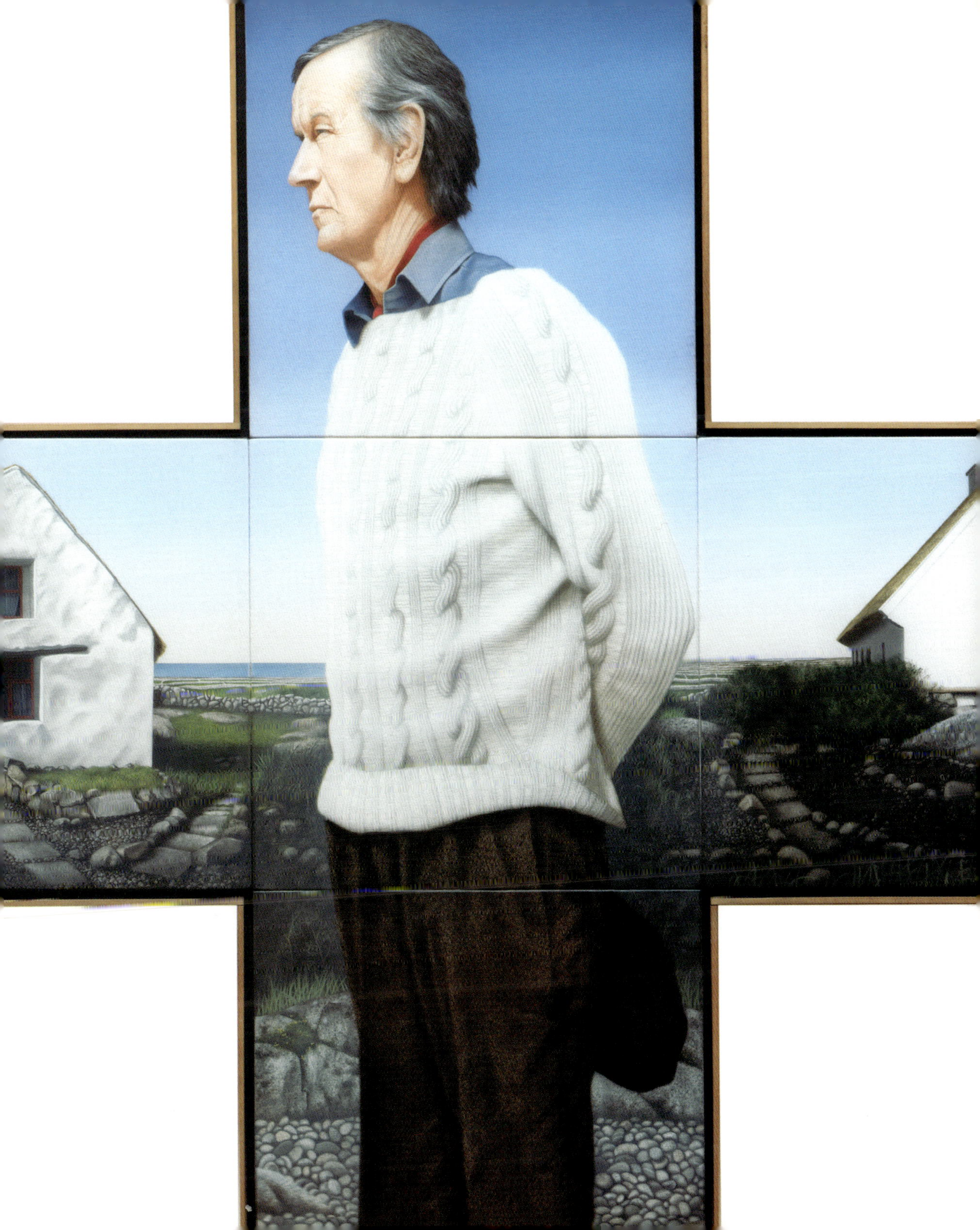

October · Deireadh Fómhair
Week 41 · Seachtain 41

8 Monday · Luan

9 Tuesday · Máirt

10 Wednesday · Céadaoin

11 Thursday · Déardaoin

12 Friday · Aoine

13 Saturday · Satharn

14 Sunday · Domhnach

Thomas Gainsborough, *A Shepherd Driving a Flock of Sheep through a Wood,* **c.1780**

Gainsborough often practised landscape painting as a pleasurable, recreational break from the demands of his portraits. His later landscape sketches were mostly imaginary scenes, produced with the aid of props such as twigs and moss, stones and coal, dried herbs and broccoli, which he arranged by candlelight in his studio. The drawings of his last years, of which this is a fine example, reveal Gainsborough as a pioneer of the Romantic movement. Through expressive strokes of chalk, ink and wash, he evokes the textures of woolly sheep and dense foliage.

M	T	W	T	F	S	S
1	2	3	4	5	6	7
8	9	10	11	12	13	14
15	16	17	18	19	20	21
22	23	24	25	26	27	28
29	30	31	1	2	3	4

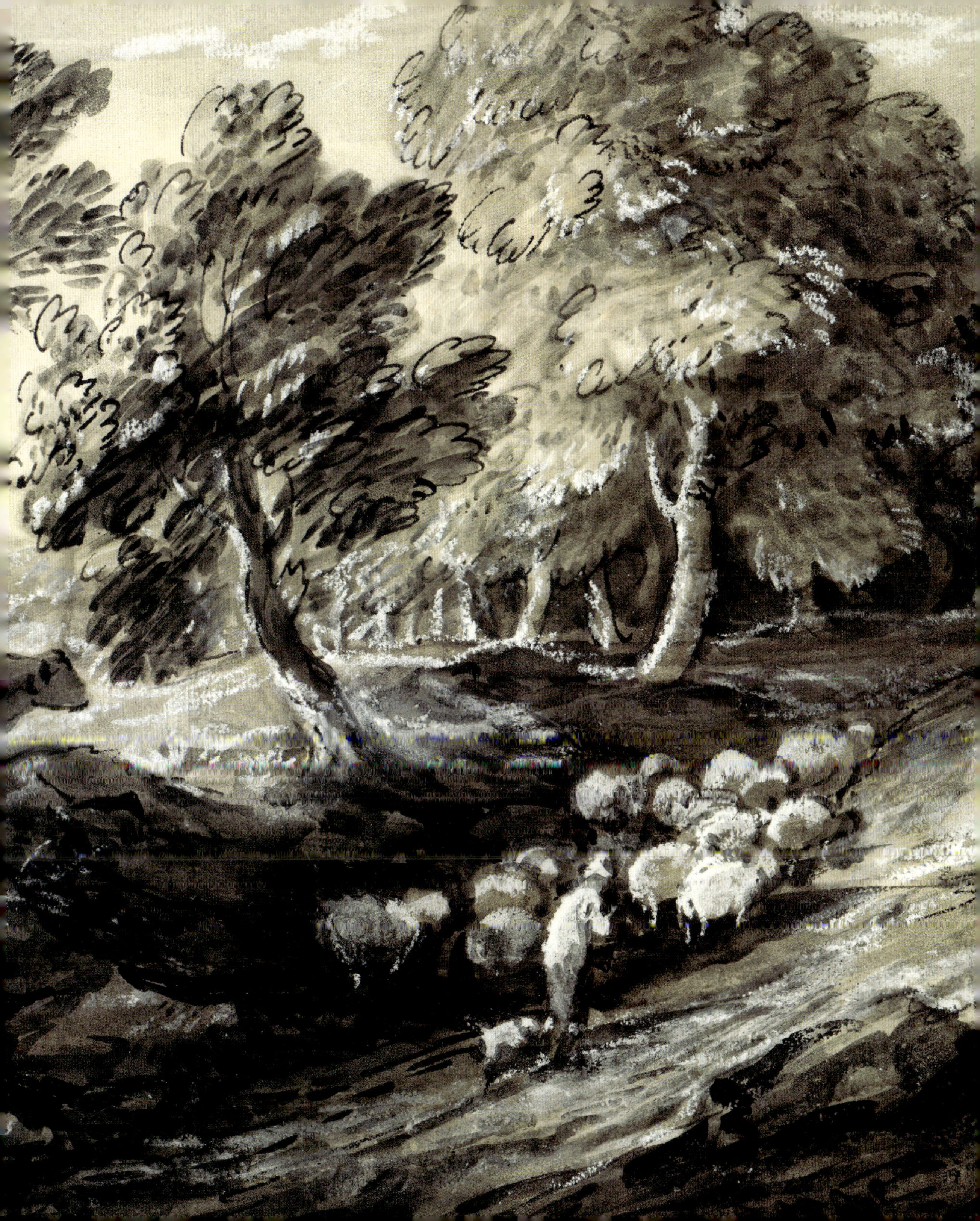

October • Deireadh Fómhair
Week 42 • Seachtain 42

15 Monday • Luan

16 Tuesday • Máirt

17 Wednesday • Céadaoin

18 Thursday • Déardaoin

19 Friday • Aoine

20 Saturday • Satharn

21 Sunday • Domhnach

Joshua Reynolds, *Caricature of Sir William Lowther and Joseph Leeson, late 1st Earl of Milltown,* **1751**
In 1751, Reynolds painted a series of satirical caricatures for the Leeson family and their friends. Here a tall and ungainly Joseph Leeson presents himself as qualified to judge the authenticity of a medal or gem hidden in his left hand using a magnifying glass. He has the full attention of a very rotund Sir William Lowther, 3rd Baronet of Marske, Yorkshire, and of Holker Hall, Lancashire. Joseph Leeson became 1st Earl of Milltown and built Russborough House, County Wicklow. Both men were extremely wealthy collectors, connoisseurs and patrons of the arts.

M	T	W	T	F	S	S
1	2	3	4	5	6	7
8	9	10	11	12	13	14
15	16	17	18	19	20	21
22	23	24	25	26	27	28
29	30	31	1	2	3	4

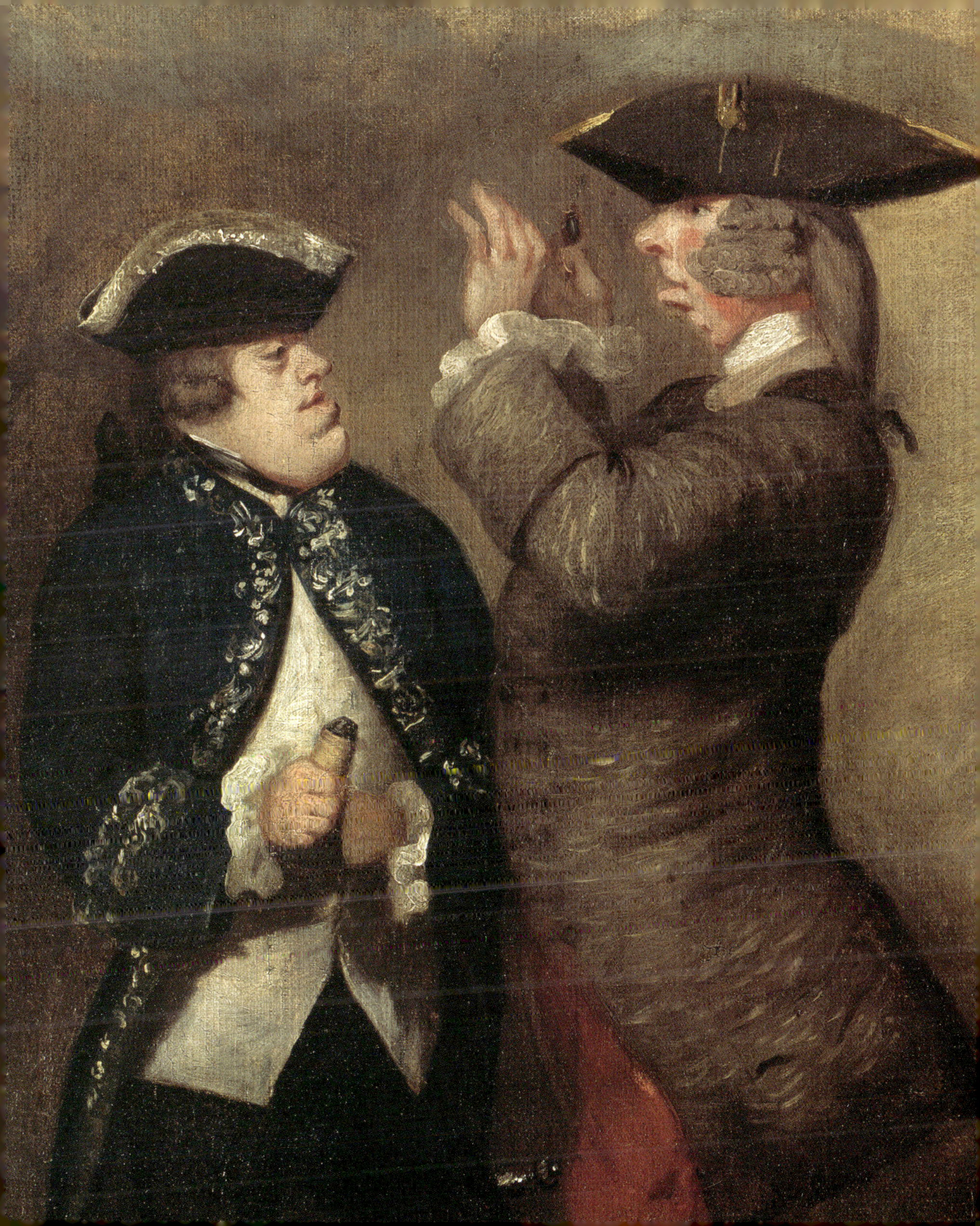

October · Deireadh Fómhair
Week 43 · Seachtain 43

22 Monday · Luan

23 Tuesday · Máirt

24 Wednesday · Céadaoin

25 Thursday · Déardaoin

26 Friday · Aoine

27 Saturday · Satharn

28 Sunday · Domhnach

Joseph Mallord William Turner, *Great Yarmouth Harbour, Norfolk,* **c.1840**

Turner visited Yarmouth on his tour of the east coast of Britain in 1824. It is not certain that he ever returned there, so consequently this watercolour, executed about sixteen years later, may have been conjured up from memory or perhaps painted from an earlier sketch. In mood and style it is similar to Turner's Venetian watercolours of the 1840s. In this romantic scene of a solitary figure contemplating a fiery sunset, the intense colours in the sky render the architectural features of the lighthouse, windmill and walled structure below less dominant.

M	T	W	T	F	S	S
1	2	3	4	5	6	7
8	9	10	11	12	13	14
15	16	17	18	19	20	21
22	23	24	25	26	27	28
29	30	31	1	2	3	4

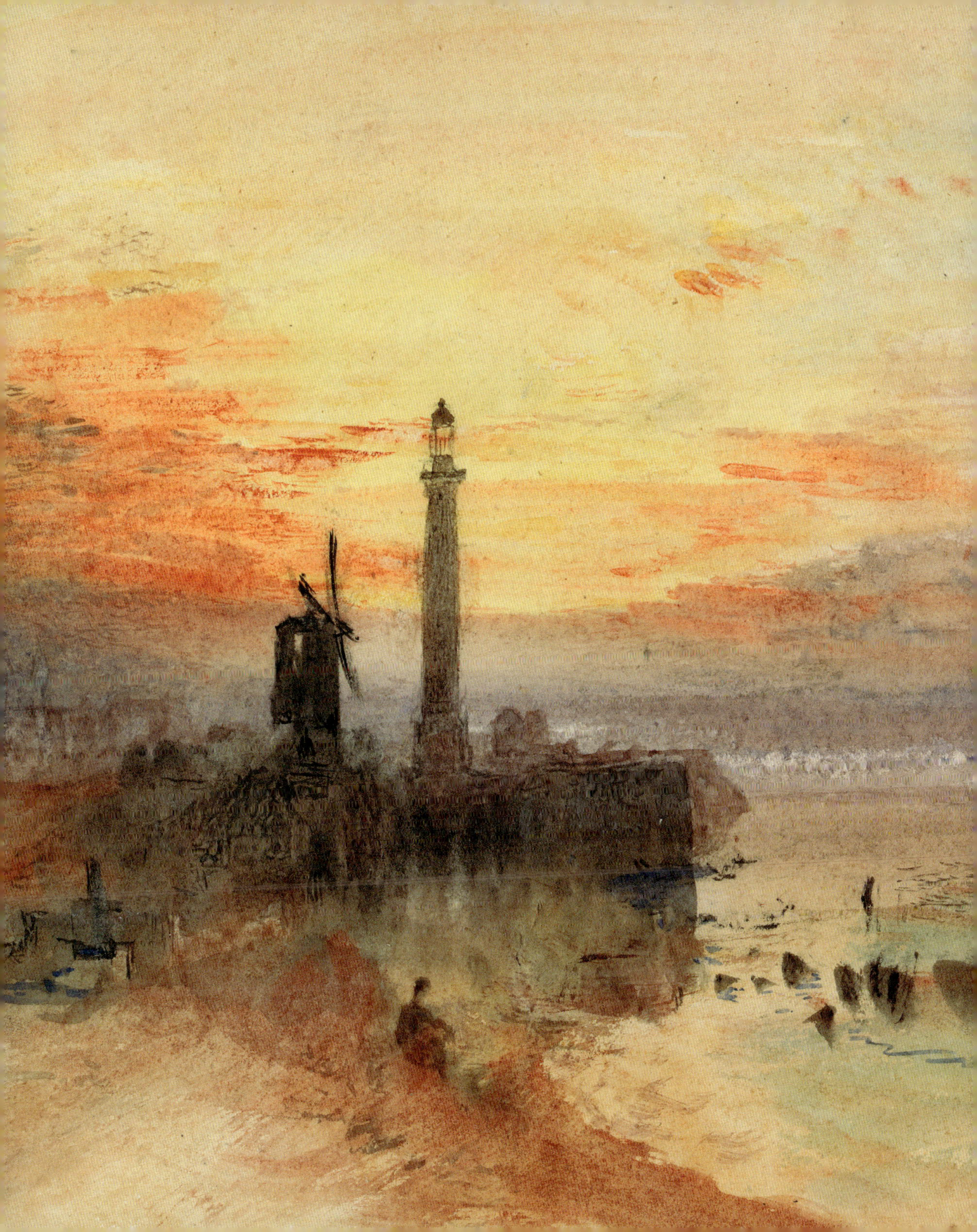

October · Deireadh Fómhair
Week 44 · Seachtain 44

29 Monday · Luan
Bank holiday (RoI)

30 Tuesday · Máirt

31 Wednesday · Céadaoin
Hallowe'en

1 Thursday · Déardaoin   November · Samhain

2 Friday · Aoine

3 Saturday · Satharn

4 Sunday · Domhnach

James Jacques Tissot, *Marguerite in Church,* **c.1861**

It was the German writer J.W. Goethe who introduced the character of Marguerite into the *Faust* legend, which Tissot painted in a series of works. Here the pensive Marguerite struggles with her crisis of faith. An image of the Last Judgement on the wall behind her, the intent prayer of the two children at the altar on the left and the void dividing them from Marguerite all heighten her sense of spiritual isolation. Costume pieces like this were typical of Tissot's early work, and he dresses Marguerite in an early 16th century hood.

M	T	W	T	F	S	S
1	2	3	4	5	6	7
8	9	10	11	12	13	14
15	16	17	18	19	20	21
22	23	24	25	26	27	28
29	30	31	1	2	3	4

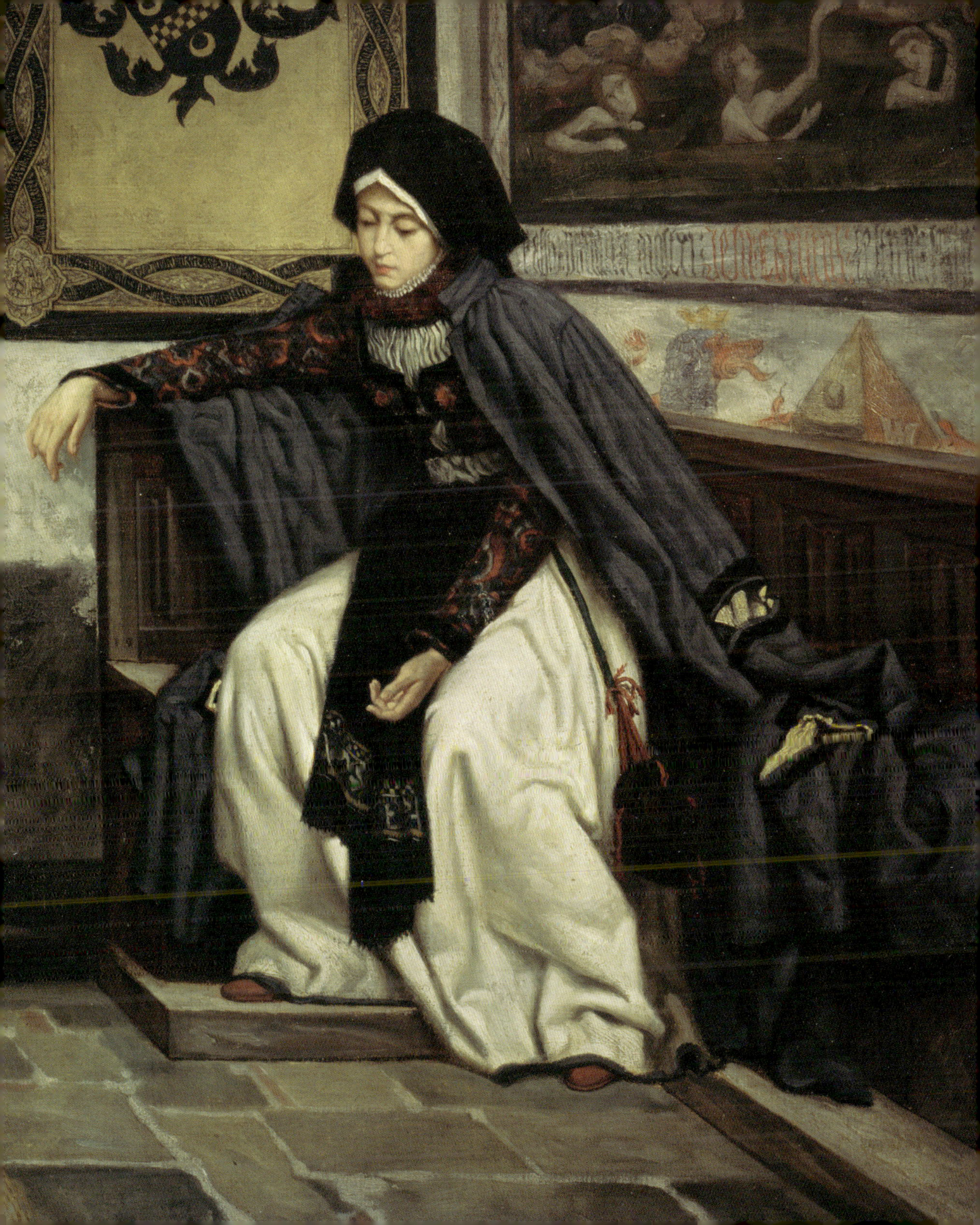

November · Samhain
Week 45 · Seachtain 45

5 Monday · Luan

6 Tuesday · Máirt

7 Wednesday · Céadaoin

8 Thursday · Déardaoin

9 Friday · Aoine

10 Saturday · Satharn

11 Sunday · Domhnach

Patrick Joseph Tuohy, *Portrait of the Honourable Biddy Campbell, Daughter of the 2nd Lord Glenavy,* **1926**

The sitter in this portrait, wearing a straw hat and a red and blue check dress, is Biddy, the daughter of Beatrice *(née* Elvery) and Gordon Campbell, Lord and Lady Glenavy. Tuohy requested so many sittings from Biddy, who was then twelve or thirteen years old, that she eventually refused to pose. This may account for her rather despondent expression, but her parents were pleased with the portrait. Biddy and her husband died in a bombing raid on London during the Second World War.

M	T	W	T	F	S	S
29	30	31	1	2	3	4
5	6	7	8	9	10	11
12	13	14	15	16	17	18
19	20	21	22	23	24	25
26	27	28	29	30	1	2

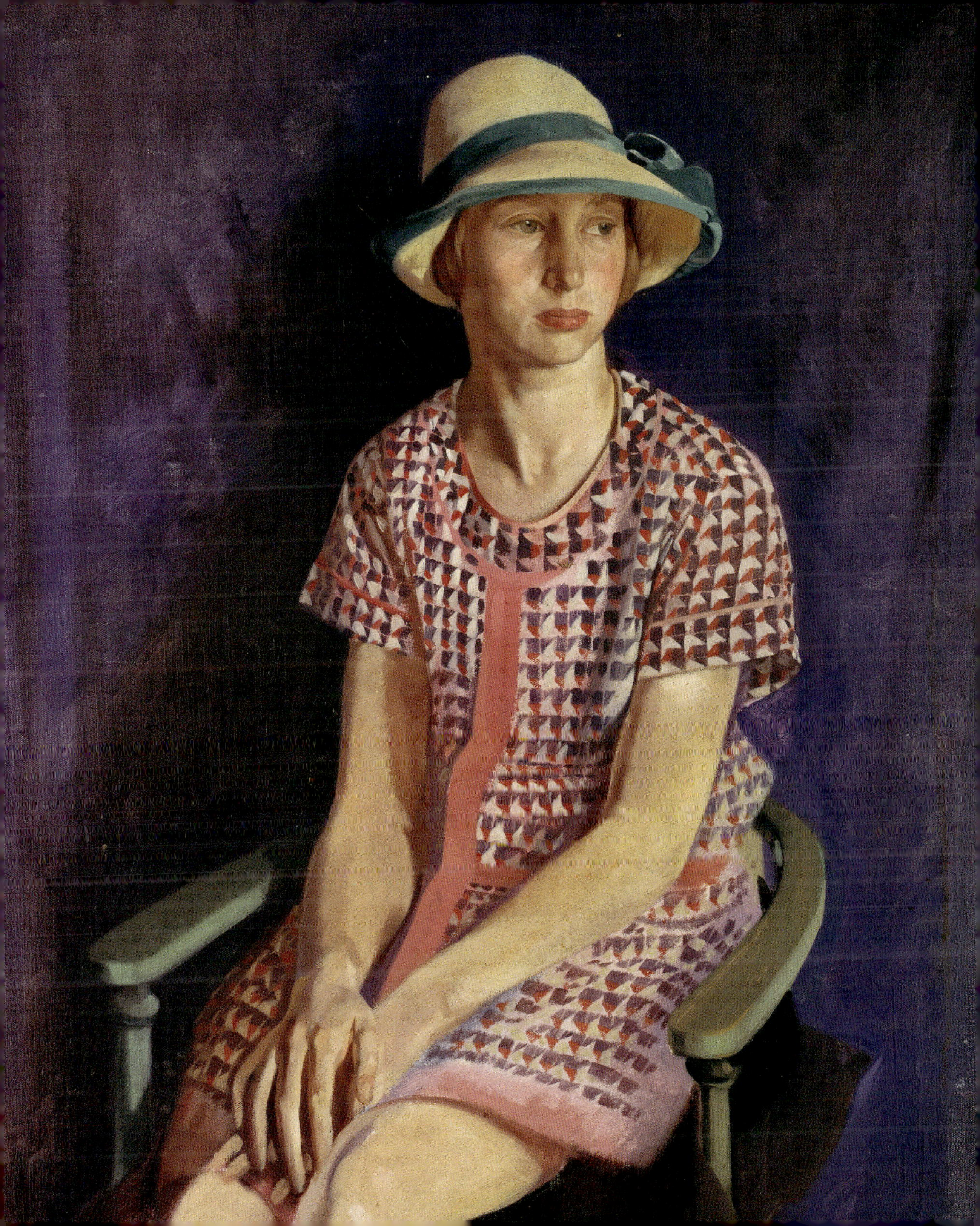

November · Samhain
Week 46 · Seachtain 46

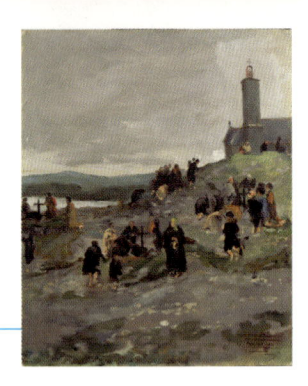

12 Monday · Luan

13 Tuesday · Máirt

14 Wednesday · Céadaoin

15 Thursday · Déardaoin

16 Friday · Aoine

17 Saturday · Satharn

18 Sunday · Domhnach

John Lavery, *Saint Patrick's Purgatory, Lough Derg,* **1929**

In August 1929, Lavery travelled to the ancient Irish pilgrimage site of Lough Derg. Contrary to his expectations, the pilgrims were not 'picturesque peasants' but 'everyday types one would see in the streets of Belfast or Dublin'. Much to his amazement, the weather was unpredictably good during his stay. In this preparatory sketch for his final painting, Lavery focuses on a group of pilgrims mingling outdoors. Beyond the bell tower of the modern basilica, one can see Lough Derg and the southern uplands of Donegal.

M	T	W	T	F	S	S
29	30	31	1	2	3	4
5	6	7	8	9	10	11
12	13	14	15	16	17	18
19	20	21	22	23	24	25
26	27	28	29	30	1	2

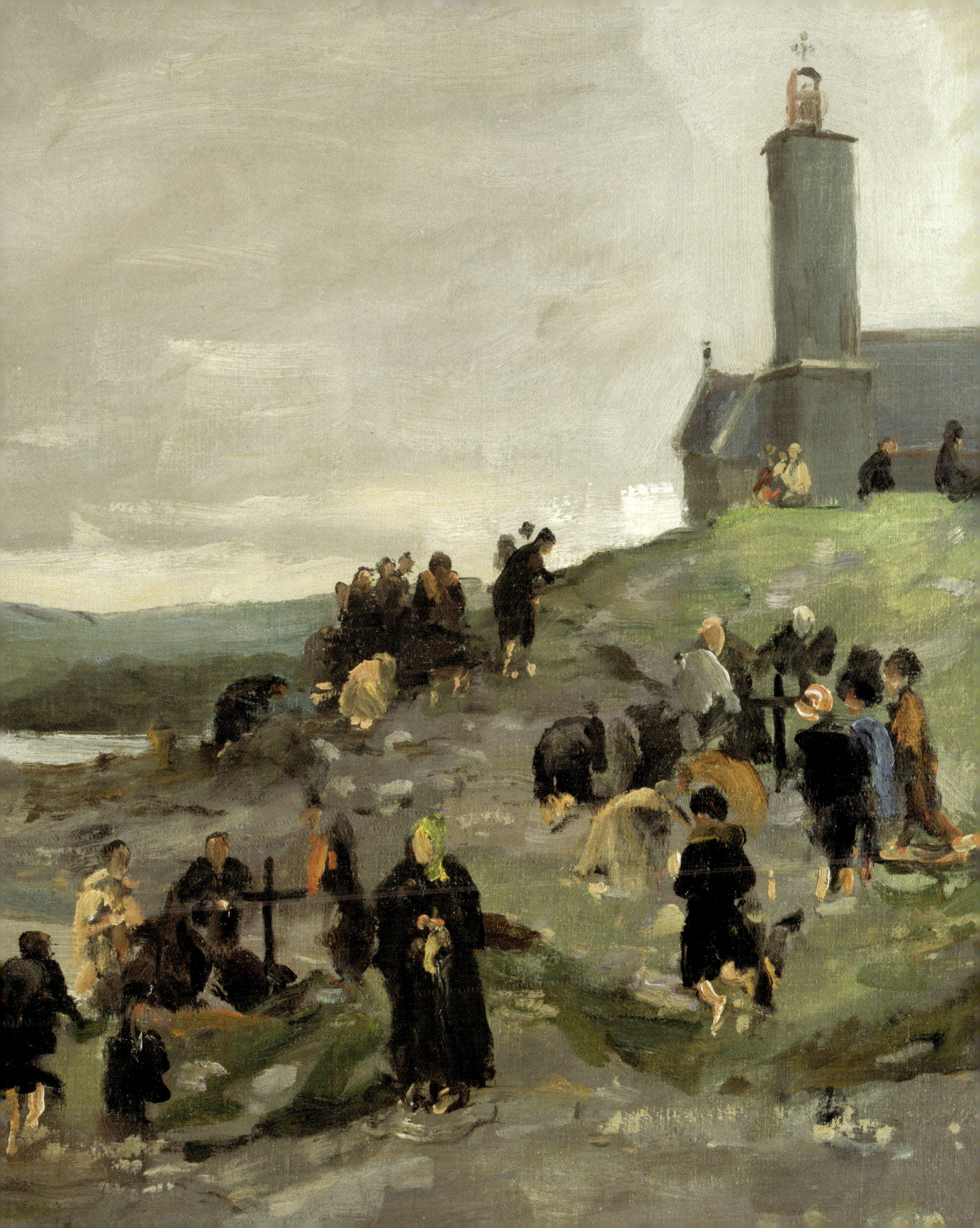

November • Samhain
Week 47 • Seachtain 47

19 Monday • Luan

20 Tuesday • Máirt

21 Wednesday • Céadaoin

22 Thursday • Déardaoin

23 Friday • Aoine

24 Saturday • Satharn

25 Sunday • Domhnach

Niall Naessens, *Rain over a Bog, after Emil Nolde,* **1997**

Many of Naessens's etchings interpret weather conditions in a precise manner, similar to that of a meteorologist. Taking as his starting point a watercolour entitled *Rain over a Marsh* by the Norwegian Expressionist Emil Nolde, which is in the Gallery's collection, Naessens has transposed Nolde's Nordic landscape into a view of Irish bogland. Sheets of unrelenting rain beat down from a turbulent and cloudy grey sky. Meticulously etched, cross-hatched lines create the atmospheric density of an overcast day, where the only hint of colour is reserved for the peat bog in the foreground.

M	T	W	T	F	S	S
29	30	31	1	2	3	4
5	6	7	8	9	10	11
12	13	14	15	16	17	18
19	20	21	22	23	24	25
26	27	28	29	30	1	2

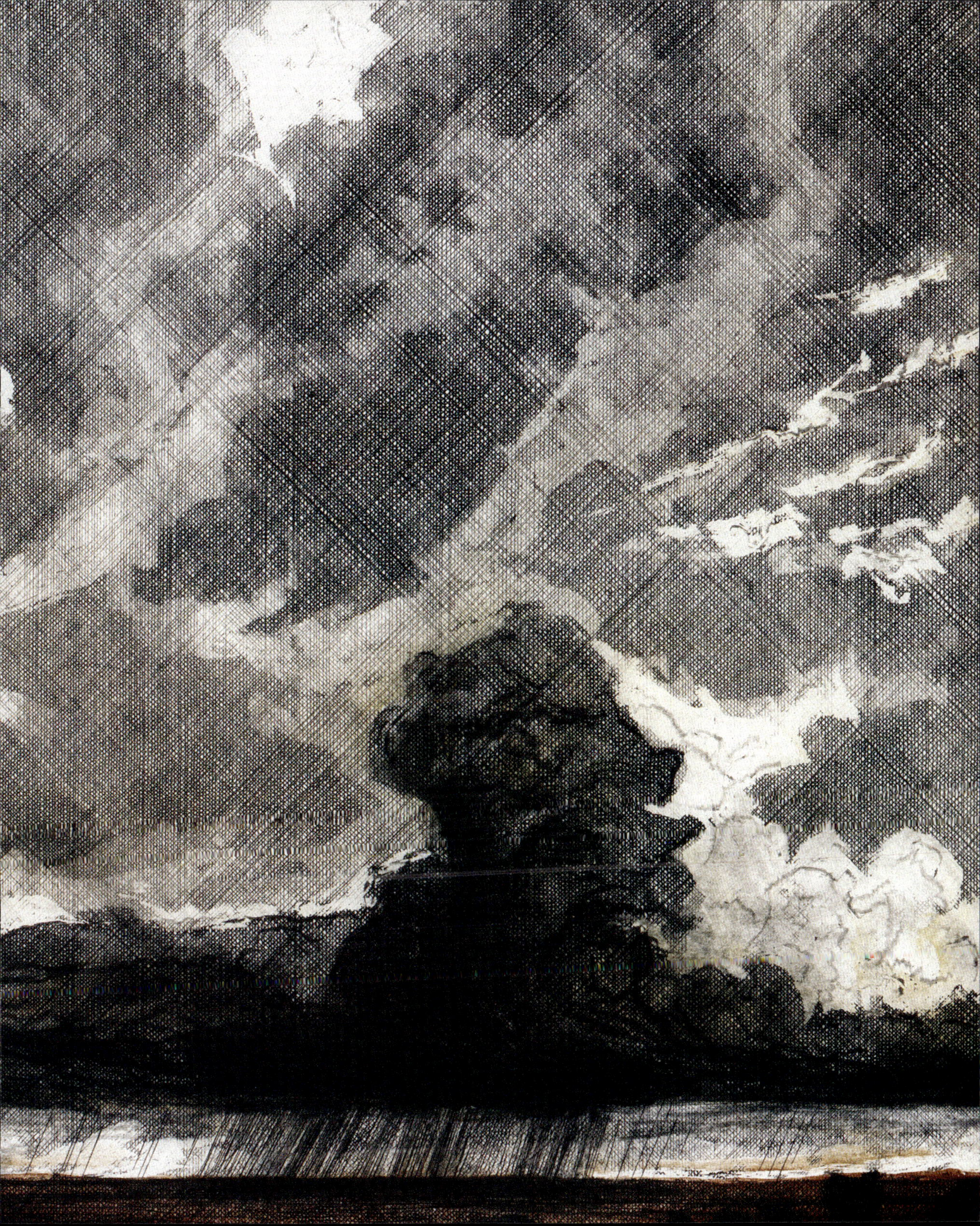

November • Samhain
Week 48 • Seachtain 48

26 Monday • Luan

27 Tuesday • Máirt

28 Wednesday • Céadaoin

29 Thursday • Déardaoin

30 Friday • Aoine
Bank holiday (Scotland)

1 Saturday • Satharn　　　　　　　　　　　　　　　　　　　December • Nollaig

2 Sunday • Domhnach

Edwin Henry Landseer, *A King Charles Spaniel,* **1840s**

Landseer was Queen Victoria's favourite painter. He specialised in portraying animals in a somewhat sentimental light and often gave them semi-human expressions, which secured his popularity during an era when sensibilities were all important. The spaniel's round face and eyes are echoed in the circular format of the picture, while its gentle, innocent expression epitomises the popular image of such a domestic animal, that of complete devotion to its master.

M	T	W	T	F	S	S
29	30	31	1	2	3	4
5	6	7	8	9	10	11
12	13	14	15	16	17	18
19	20	21	22	23	24	25
26	27	28	29	30	1	2

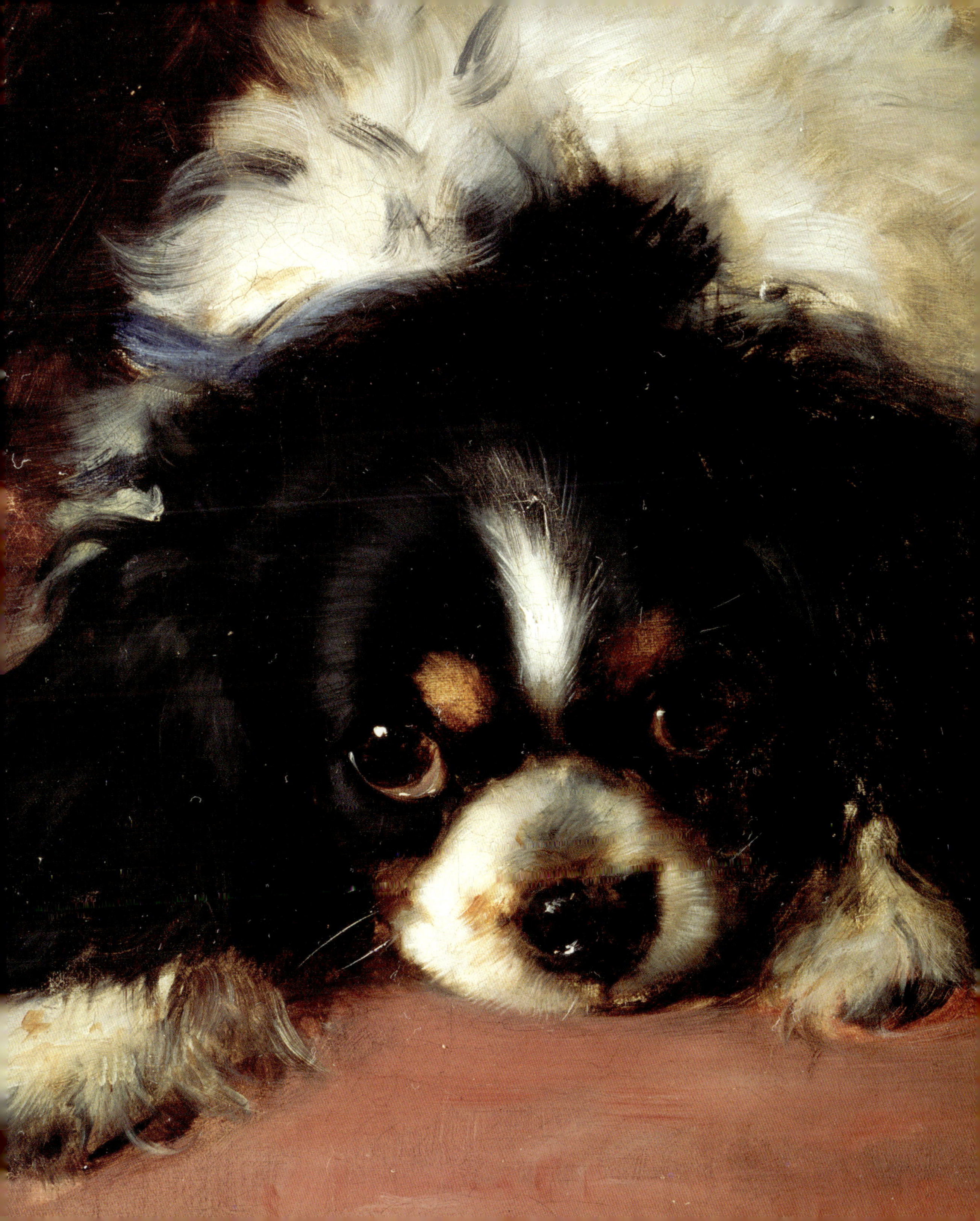

December • Nollaig
Week 49 • Seachtain 49

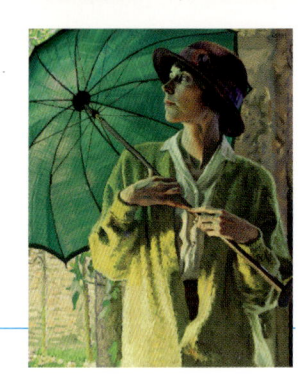

3 Monday • Luan

4 Tuesday • Máirt

5 Wednesday • Céadaoin

6 Thursday • Déardaoin

7 Friday • Aoine

8 Saturday • Satharn

9 Sunday • Domhnach

William John Leech, *The Sunshade,* **c.1913**

This is a painting of the artist's first wife, Elizabeth Kerlin, whom he married in 1912. Leech produced numerous portraits of Elizabeth, often affording her an elegant but rather enigmatic quality. In this case, sunlight bursts in from the left, illuminating her profile and following the contours of her graceful hands. The cadmium yellow of her cardigan is vibrant against the viridian green of her sunshade, which casts green shadows onto her shoulders. Darker tones are introduced through her hair and the red, purple and lilac of her hat.

M	T	W	T	F	S	S
26	27	28	29	30	1	2
3	4	5	6	7	8	9
10	11	12	13	14	15	16
17	18	19	20	21	22	23
24	25	26	27	28	29	30
31	1	2	3	4	5	6

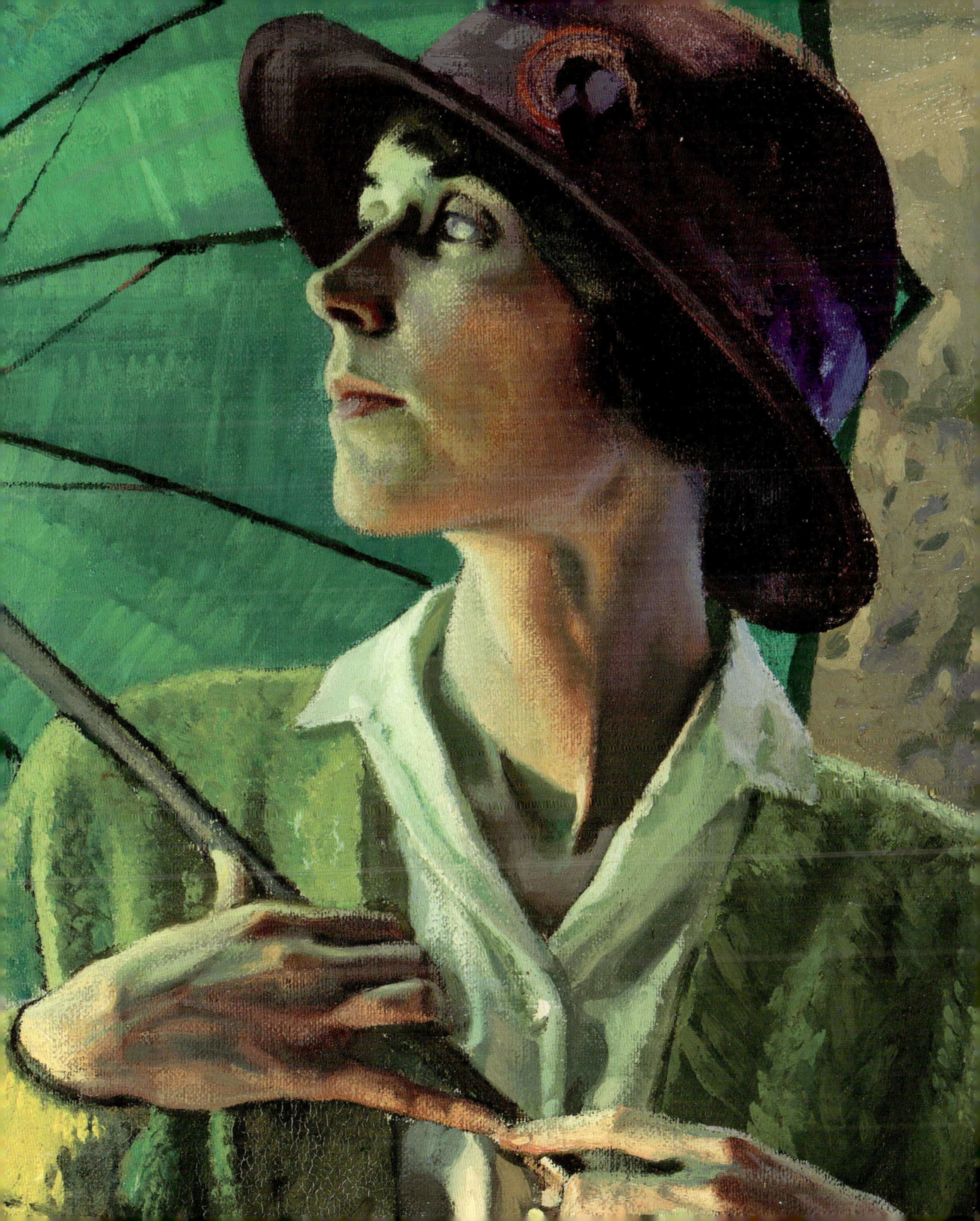

December • Nollaig
Week 50 • Seachtain 50

10 Monday • Luan

11 Tuesday • Máirt

12 Wednesday • Céadaoin

13 Thursday • Déardaoin

14 Friday • Aoine

15 Saturday • Satharn

16 Sunday • Domhnach

Anne Yeats, *Women and Washing, Sicily,* **1965–1966**

Anne Yeats, daughter of William Butler Yeats, was inspired to create this work by a trip to Sicily in 1965. Three Sicilian women are depicted resting from their domestic chores. Although close together, they seem absorbed in their own thoughts. Many of Yeats's figure studies focused on women and themes of loneliness and isolation. Areas of cool shadow contrast with bright light in the open street and the laundry that dries in the heat of the sun.

M	T	W	T	F	S	S
26	27	28	29	30	1	2
3	4	5	6	7	8	9
10	11	12	13	14	15	16
17	18	19	20	21	22	23
24	25	26	27	28	29	30
31	1	2	3	4	5	6

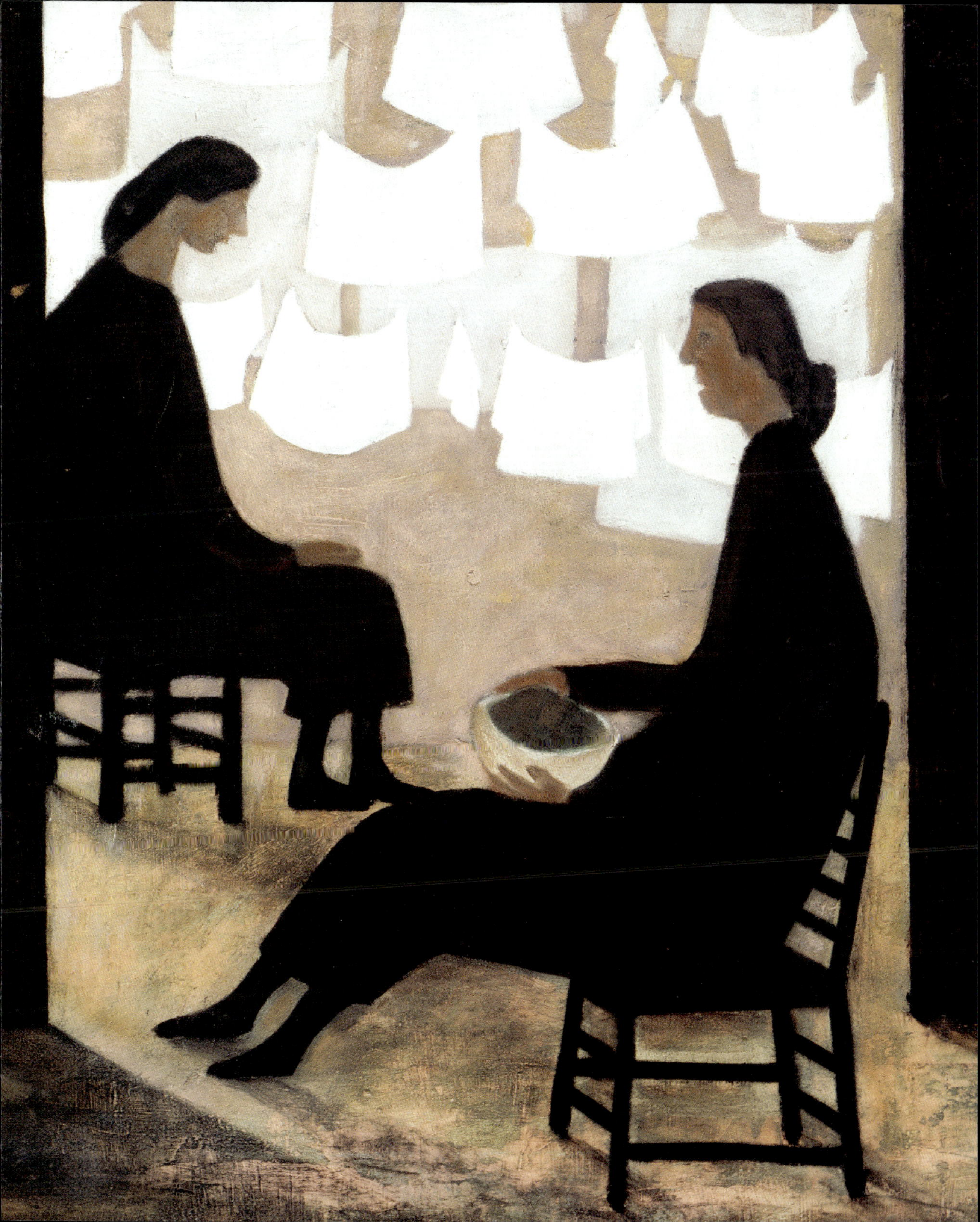

December • Nollaig
Week 51 • Seachtain 51

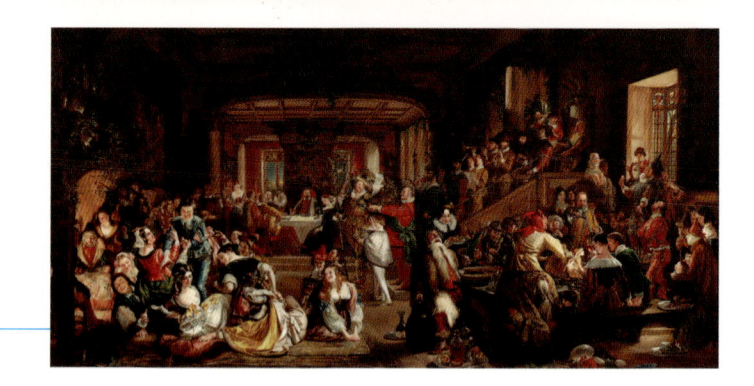

17 Monday • Luan

18 Tuesday • Máirt

19 Wednesday • Céadaoin

20 Thursday • Déardaoin

21 Friday • Aoine

22 Saturday • Satharn

23 Sunday • Domhnach

Daniel Maclise, *Merry Christmas in the Baron's Hall,* **1838**

In the interior of a large Jacobean hall, Christmas is celebrated with festivity and abandon. A boar's head, decorated with bay and rosemary, is served on a silver platter while the Lord of Misrule chants a carol in its praise. Father Christmas mixes the wassails (spiced ale or mulled wine) while Saint Distaff hands him the roasted pippins that will be served with them. Also enjoying the banquet are Saint George and the dragon, a Turk, a jester on a hobby horse, a juggler, a fiddler and numerous choristers, musicians and revellers.

M	T	W	T	F	S	S
26	27	28	29	30	1	2
3	4	5	6	7	8	9
10	11	12	13	14	15	16
17	18	19	20	21	22	23
24	25	26	27	28	29	30
31	1	2	3	4	5	6

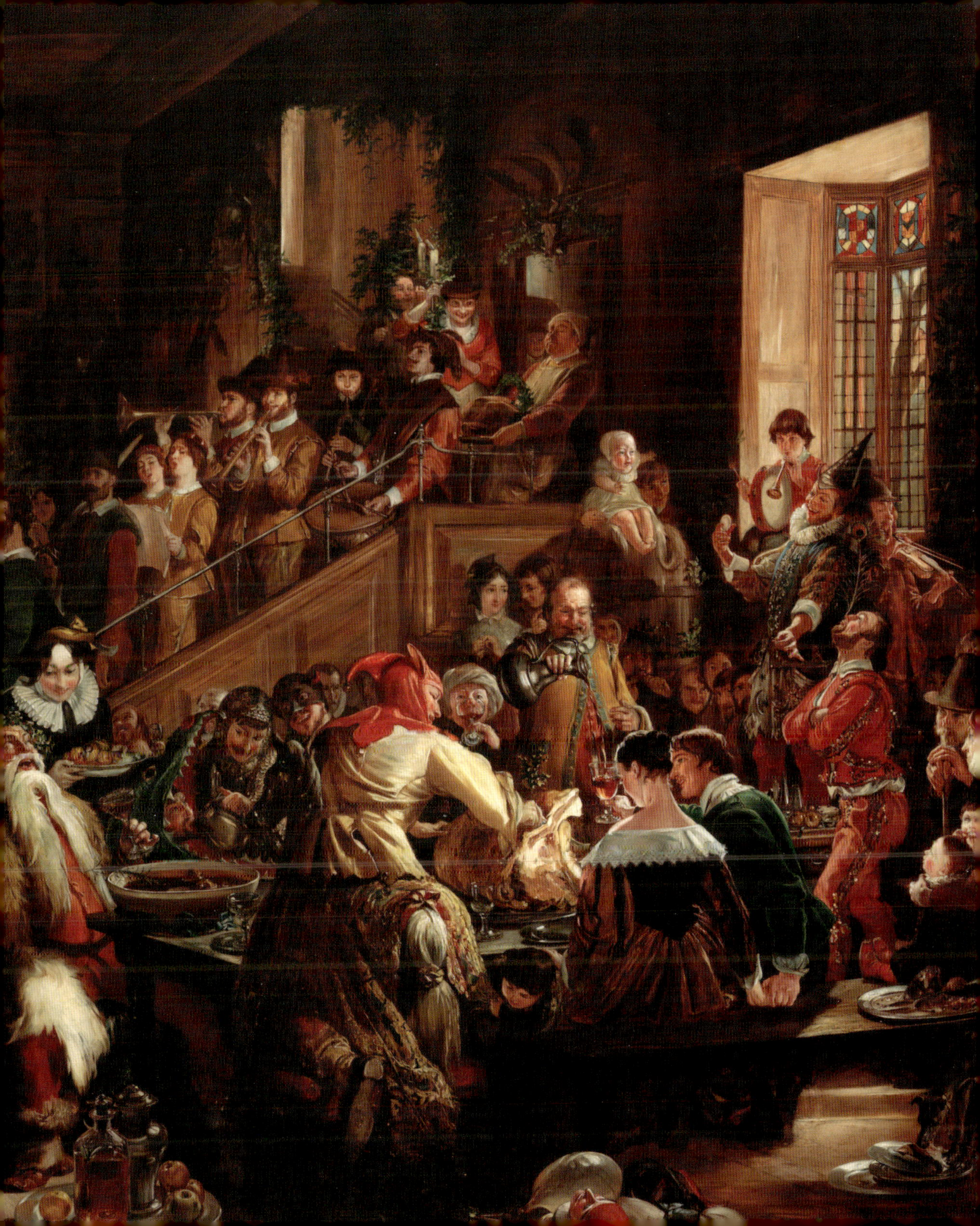

December · Nollaig
Week 52 · Seachtain 52

24 Monday · Luan
Christmas Eve

25 Tuesday · Máirt
Christmas Day

26 Wednesday · Céadaoin
St Stephen's Day

27 Thursday · Déardaoin

28 Friday · Aoine

29 Saturday · Satharn

30 Sunday · Domhnach

31 Monday · Luan
New Year's Eve

Frederic William Burton, *The Virgin and Child with Angels,* **19th century**

Burton painted in watercolour using a meticulous technique, employing rich colours whose density often resembles that of oil paint. This painting reveals the influence of Early Renaissance altarpieces in the flat, gold background, the attention to detail, the symmetrical composition, the Virgin's facial features and the diminutive size of the angels who crown the Virgin as Queen of Heaven. Burton greatly admired the work of Flemish and German painters of the Early Renaissance, as well as the English Pre-Raphaelites of the mid-19th century, whose choice of medieval subjects often influenced him.

M	T	W	T	F	S	S
26	27	28	29	30	1	2
3	4	5	6	7	8	9
10	11	12	13	14	15	16
17	18	19	20	21	22	23
24	25	26	27	28	29	30
31	1	2	3	4	5	6

List of Works

Govaert Flinck, 1615-1660
Bathsheba's appeal to David,
Dutch, 1651
Oil on canvas
NGI 64

Ludolf Backhuysen I, 1630-1708,
The Arrival of the 'Kattendijk' at Texel, 22 July 1702, 1702
Oil on canvas
Unframed: 133 x 111 cm
NGI 173

Seán O'Sullivan, 1906-1964
Portrait of Douglas Hyde, President of Ireland (1860-1949), Poet and Scholar, Irish, 20th Century, Oil on canvas
Unframed: 128 x 102 cm
© Artist's Estate
NGI 101

Nicolas Lancret, 1690-1743
La Malice (Mischief), French, c.1735, Oil on canvas,
Unframed: 36 x 29 cm
NGI 802

Paul Henry 1876-1958, *The Potato Diggers,*
1912, Oil on canvas,
Unframed: 51 x 46 cm
NGI 1870

Dante Gabriel Rossetti,
1828-1882, *Jane Burden (1840-1914),* 1858, Ink, graphite and wash with white highlights on paper,
Unframed: 48.3 x 35.3 cm
NGI 2259

Canaletto, 1697-1768, *Saint Mark's Square, Venice,* c.1756,
Oil on canvas,
Unframed: 46 x 77 cm
NGI 286

Moyra Barry, 1886-1960
Self-Portrait in the Artist's Studio, 1920, Oil on canvas
Unframed: 30.4 x 25.5 cm
© Artist's Estate.
NGI 4366

George Leslie Hunter, 1877-1931
Still Life with Dahlias, Wine Glass and Fruit, c.1913, Oil on canvas
Unframed: 61 x 50.8 cm
NGI 2006.22

Daniel Maclise, 1806-1870
The Marriage of Strongbow and Aoife, Irish, c.1854, Oil on canvas
Unframed: 315 x 513 cm
NGI 205

Willem Claesz. Heda, 1594-1680
A Banquet-piece, c.1635, Oil on wood panel
Unframed: 55.3 x 73.8 cm
NGI 514

Zanobi di Jacopo Machiavelli, 1418-1479
Virgin and Child Enthroned with Saints, c.1470, Tempera on wood panel
Unframed: 132.5 x 148.7 cm
NGI 108

Mick O'Dea, b.1958
Portrait of Brian Friel (b.1929),
2009, Oil on canvas
Unframed: 60.5 x 50.5 cm
© Mick O'Dea. All Rights Reserved, IVARO 2011
NGI 2009.25

Dominicus van Wijnen, b.1661, fl.1690, *The Temptation of Saint Anthony,* 1680s
Oil on canvas
Unframed: 72 x 72 cm
NGI 527

Harry Clarke, 1889-1931
The Wild Swans, 1915, Ink and watercolour, with bodycolour highlights on paper
Unframed: 30.5 x 21 cm
NGI 2008.89.5

Pierre Bonnard, 1867-1947
Nude before a Mirror, 1915
Oil on canvas
Unframed: 59.9 x 51 cm
© ADAGP, Paris and DACS, London 2011
NGI 2009.13

Nathaniel Hone II, 1831-1917
Pastures at Malahide,
c.1894-1896, Oil on canvas
Unframed: 82 x 124 cm
NGI 588

Studio of Peter Paul Rubens,
1577-1640, *The Annunciation,*
Previously attributed to Peter Paul Rubens, 1577-1640, Flemish, 1614, Oil on oak panel
Unframed: 186 x 153.9 cm
NGI 60

François Boucher, 1703-1770
A Female Nude Reclining on a Chaise-Longue, c.1752, Graphite, red and white chalk on brown paper
Unframed: 22.2 x 36.2 cm
NGI 2007.3

José Antolínez, 1635-1676
The Liberation of Saint Peter,
early 1670s, Oil on canvas
Unframed: 167 x 128 cm
NGI 31

Matthew James Lawless,
1837-1864, *An Angling Party,*
c.1860,
Oil on canvas,
Unframed: 40.5 x 61.5 cm
NGI 2008.98

Attributed to Steven van der Meulen, 1543-1568, *Portrait of Thomas Butler, 10th Earl of Ormond,* 1560s, Oil on panel
Unframed: 93 x 68 cm.
NGI 4687

Léon-Augustin Lhermitte,
1844-1925
Harvesters at Rest, 1888,
Oil on canvas
Unframed: 96 x 75 cm
NGI 4255

Thomas Roberts, 1748-1777
A View of Ballyshannon, County Donegal, 18th century
Oil on canvas
Unframed: 45.4 x 64 cm
NGI 4701

Joseph Mallord William Turner,
1775-1851
Beech Trees at Norbury Park, Surrey, British, c.1797
Graphite and watercolour on sheet lined with laid paper
Unframed: 44 x 43.1 cm.
NGI 2409

Sarah Henrietta Purser,
1848-1943, *A Lady Holding a Doll's Rattle,* 1885, Oil on canvas
Unframed: 41 x 31 cm
© Artist's Estate
NGI 4131

John Luke, 1906-1975
Shaw's Bridge, c. 1934
Linocut on Japanese paper
Image: 26.2 x 36.5 cm
© Artist's Estate
NGI 2008.86

Edwin Hayes, 1820-1904
An Emigrant Ship, Dublin Bay, Sunset, Irish, 1853, Oil on canvas
Unframed: 58 x 86 cm
NGI 1209

Harry Andersson, 1895-1948
Aladdin, 1923, Woodcut
Sheet: 40 x 30cm © DACS 2011
NGI 20928

William Orpen, 1878-1931
The Wash House, 1905, Oil on canvas
Unframed: 91 x 73 cm
NGI 946

Paul Henry, 1876-1958
Launching the Curragh,
1910-1911
NGI 1869

Robert Ponsonby Staples,
1853-1943, *Ireland's Eye from Howth,* 1899, Graphite, pastel, chalk and watercolour on paper
Unframed: 26.3 x 35.5 cm
NGI 2009.16

Matthew James Lawless,
1837-1864, *A Sick Call,* 1863,
Oil on canvas
Unframed: 63 x 103 cm
NGI 864

Guercino, 1591-1666, *The Virgin and Child (for the Madonna del Carmine Presenting a Scapular to a Carmelite, in Cento's Pinacoteca Civica,* c.1615
Red chalk on beige paper
Unframed: 20 x 17.8 cm
NGI 2603

Thomas Hickey, 1741-1824
Portrait of two Children, 1769
Oil on canvas
Unframed: 98 x 80 cm
NGI 863

Aloysius O'Kelly, 1853-1936
Preparing for Winter, 1880s
Oil on canvas
Unframed: 61.1 x 50.6 cm
NGI 2009.15

Pieter de Hooch, 1629-after 1684, *Players at Tric-trac,*
c.1652-1655, Oil on wood panel
Unframed: 45 x 33.5 cm)
NGI 322

Hugh Douglas Hamilton,
1740-1808, *Cupid and Psyche,*
c.1792, Pen and brown ink with white bodycolour and graphite on paper, sheet: 32 x 25.5 cm
NGI 19617

James Arthur O'Connor,
1792-1841, *A Thunderstorm: The Frightened Wagoner,* 1832, Oil on canvas
Unframed: 63.7 x 76.7 cm
NGI 4041

David Woodlock, 1842-1929
Portrait of Cardinal John Henry Newman, (1801-1890), c.1888
Oil on canvas
Unframed: 53.3 x 43.1 cm
NGI 4525

Robert Ballagh, b.1943
Portrait of Noel Browne (1915-1997), Politician, 1985
Oil on canvas
Unframed: 183 x 137 cm
© The Artist
NGI 4573

Thomas Gainsborough,
1727-1788
A Shepherd Driving a Flock of Sheep through a Wood, c.1780
Black and white chalk, ink and wash on paper
Unframed: 27.4 x 36.2 cm
NGI 2115

Joshua Reynolds, 1723-1792
Caricature of Sir William Lowther and Joseph Leeson, late 1st Earl of Milltown, 1751, Oil on canvas
Unframed: 75 x 53 cm
NGI 735

Joseph Mallord William Turner,
1775-1851, *Great Yarmouth Harbour, Norfolk,* British, c.1840
Watercolour with scraping out on ivory wove paper
Unframed: 25 x 36.6 cm
NGI 2425

James Jacques Tissot, 1836-1902
Marguerite in Church, c.1861
NGI 4280

Patrick Joseph Tuohy, 1894-1930
Portrait of Biddy Campbell, Daughter of the 2nd Lord Glenavy, 20th century, Oil on canvas, Unframed: 54 x 32 cm
NGI 4027

John Lavery, 1856-1941
Saint Patrick's Purgatory, Lough Derg, 20th century, Oil on canvas on board, Unframed:
60.5 x 50.5 cm, by courtesy of Felix Rosenstiel's Widow & Son Ltd., London on behalf of the Estate of Sir John Lavery
NGI 4666

Niall Naessens, b. 1961
Rain over a Bog, after Emil Nolde, 1997, Etching on Velin Arche Blanc Paper Sheet:
65.5 x 30cm, © The Artist
NGI 20883

Edwin Henry Landseer,
1802-1873
A King Charles Spaniel, 1840s,
Oil on canvas, Unframed:
35 x 35 cm
NGI 4333

William John Leech, 1881-1968
The Sunshade, Irish, c.1913, Oil on canvas, Unframed: 81 x 65 cm
© Artist's Estate
NGI 1246

Anne Yeats, 1919-2001
Women and Washing, Sicily,
1965-1966, Oil on paper
Unframed: 38 x 57 cm
© Estate of Anne Yeats. All rights reserved, DACS 2011
NGI 4613

Daniel Maclise, 1806-1870
Merry Christmas in the Baron's Hall, Irish, 1838, Oil on canvas,
Unframed: 183 x 366 cm
NGI 156

Frederic William Burton,
1816-1900, *The Virgin and Child with Angels,* 19th century, gold paint and watercolour on card
Unframed: 53.4 x 38 cm
NGI 7475

Additional credits

FRONT COVER
Robert Ponsonby Staples,
(1853-1943), *On the Beach, Broadstairs, Kent,* 1899, Oil on canvas, Irish School
NGI 4712.

BACK COVER
Paul Henry, 1876-1958
A Connemara Village, 20th century, Oil on canvas
Unframed: 76.2 x 91.4 cm
NGI 4734

Page 1:
Francis Wheatley, 1747-1801
Child with a Dog, 18th century
Oil on canvas
Unframed: 69 cm
NGI 374

Page 2:
Jules Joseph Lefebvre, 1836-1911, *Lauretta,* 1870s-1880s

Page 5:
Nicolaes Maes, 1634-1693
Vertumnus and Pomona, 1673
Oil on wood panel
Unframed: 48.5 x 60.4 cm
NGI 347

ENDPAPERS
Guercino, 1591-1666, *The Virgin and Child (for the Madonna del Carmine Presenting a Scapular to a Carmelite, in Cento's Pinacoteca Civica,* c.1615
Red chalk on beige paper
Unframed: 20 x 17.8 cm
NGI 2603

All photographs are © National Gallery of Ireland unless stated otherwise.